The Many Waters

"And the Spirit of God moved upon the face of the waters"

Lauretta Lueck

ROSETTA STONE PRESS

Published by Rosetta Stone Press
Calgary, Alberta, CANADA

Internet: http://www.themanywaters.com
E-mail: info@themanywaters.com

Canadian Cataloguing in Publication Data

Lueck, Lauretta, 1934–
The many waters

Includes bibliographical references and index.
ISBN: 0–9687090–0–1

1. Water in the Bible. 2. Bible. O.T. Genesis—Criticism, interpretation, etc. I. Title.
BS1199.W22L83 2000 221.6'4 C00–910793–2

CREDITS:
Cover Illustration: *Large Magellanic Cloud*, Eyewire, Digital Vision 028308
Copyediting by Wayne Magnuson, Calgary, Alberta
Interior and Cover Design by Jeremy Drought, Last Impression Publishing Service, Calgary, Alberta
Indexing by Judy Dunlop, Edmonton, Alberta
Printed and bound in Canada by Friesens, Altona, Manitoba

DEDICATION

To our shimmery blue-green planet.
Just one of the many waters.

As a result of an immense amount of research that has been carried out in the field, the study, and the laboratory, our own generation is aware of more aspects of the distant past than were dreamed of by our great-grandfathers and their fathers. Much that was long accepted as implausible myth or poetic allegory has been substantiated.[1]

[1] Cottrell, L. (1962). *The Horizon Book of Lost Worlds.* New York, NY: American Heritage Publishing Co., p. 6.

ACKNOWLEDGMENTS

I would like to thank my adult children for their encouragement during the writing of this manuscript and especially to my daughter Cherry and son-in-law Brian, for taking on the secretarial and computer tasks, and all the errands that were required to complete the project.

I also appreciate the guidance given to me by Johanna Bates, and for the invaluable work in the design and production of the book by Jeremy Drought. Our thanks are extended to Judy Dunlop for her production of the index—a labour intensive task—in a timely and professional manner. And I can't forget my cheerful publicist, Joni Hamilton whose enthusiasm was contagious, and Wayne Magnuson, my editor, who suggested that Handl's *Water Music* be recommended listening while reading *The Many Waters*.

The Rosicrucian Society acknowledged my request to quote from the *Book of Jasher*, as did Kessinger Publishing from *Pistis Sophia*, by G.R.S. Mead. I thank them for their generosity and for their foresight in preserving these ancient writings for posterity and the good of humankind.

Foreword

ONE day, more than thirty years ago, I was reading from a book on science when the words "ours is a watery planet" seemed to stand out on the page. Of course I knew that our world was almost two thirds covered in water, but at that moment it struck a cord since I had read similar descriptions in the bible.

Ours is a watery planet. THAT WAS IT! In the Bible, the symbol for life is water. All living things have to have water, and all that lives is mostly made of water. It would seem natural then that wherever there is water there would be life of some kind. It is a perfect symbol. The Bible speaks of there being "many waters" in the heavens, and there are "peoples and nations and tongues."

We are not alone, and I was intrigued! Persistently, I searched the Good Book for other hidden treasures that we may have lost through misinterpretation. I found more than I had expected to find and, for the next year, I indulged myself in gathering notes on bits of paper and storing them in a cardboard box in a drawer.

My life, until then, had been a Christian one, which means that I no longer attend church services. I was born into an evangelical Baptist home and firmly believed in God, and in a heaven and a hell. Nevertheless, since early childhood, I have also been interested in the natural sciences; especially in astronomy, archeology and paleontology. Despite the church's teachings, I furtively believed that the world was millions of years old, dinosaurs once roamed the earth, and that we are primates. I also believed that the Bible was the Word of God which supposedly contradicted the theory of evolution. What was the truth?

Three decades passed and I was an enthusiastic fan of the space program and its search for life. We were seeing the dawn of a New Age, with new thoughts, ideas and discoveries.

The coming of the 21st century, however, has also brought turmoil between religion and science. Ignorance has once again raised it's head as Christians in America demand that their children believe in a six day creation and that God came down and molded man out of mud. And we again have with us the prophets of doom—who predict the world will end sometime in the year 2000.

It was time to retrieve the old cardboard box and, in 1998, I began to write *The Many Waters*.

Lauretta E. Lueck
Calgary, Alberta
May 2000

AUTHOR'S NOTE

Unless stated otherwise, all verses of scripture appearing in this book are quoted from the *King James Authorized Version of the Bible*. Because this Bible is written in the English of 1611, I have taken the liberty of changing some of its words into more contemporary English—for easier reading, i.e; *said* instead of *saith*, *you* instead of *thou*, etc. There is nothing sacred about Shakespearean English.

Although I am proudly Canadian, wherever there is a difference in Canadian and American spelling, I have chosen the American way. I believe in simplicity and that someday all English words should be reviewed and modified.

CONTENTS

Introduction

> I do not know what I may appear to the world, but to myself I seem to have been only like a boy playing on the seashore, and diverting myself in now and then finding a smoother pebble or a prettier shell than ordinary, whilst the great ocean of truth lay all undiscovered before me.
>
> —Isaac Newton

I too have been strolling along the shores of time, shuffling through the sands of ancient writings, legends and mythology, and have picked up, here and there, some interesting pebbles and shells. Some of these gems of truth have lain buried deep in allegory and symbolism for centuries, and even millennia, and some have been right out there on the surface, kicked about and walked on, their value unrecognized.

The Bible of today is a compilation of ancient manuscripts by men who "spoke as they were moved by the Holy Spirit." So it is written. Then, centuries later, there were the translators and the languages they had to decipher—a labor of love, as they too were moved by the Spirit. Finally, over many more years were the men who had to decide which of the old writings should be included in the canon that would become the Word of God. They were kings, rulers and leaders of politics and religion who all had their own agendas and reasons for their choices. Through it all, it's a miracle that we even have a Bible, but it's not perfect. It evolved down through the ages with humankind and is written by human hands, and there is a great deal of sand to be sifted through. The gems of truth are not always on the surface.

My findings are based only on *The King James Version of the Bible* and supported with ancient writings from parchments, scrolls and tablets of stone. No other contemporary Bible had the answers in my quest for truth.

In 1881, some biblical scholars decided to make the Bible more accessible and easier to read and understand by translating it into Modern English. Their motives were honorable, but in the process they unwittingly deleted much of the symbolism and allegory. *The Revised Version of the English Bible*, and those that followed, are fine for general reading, but lost to us are the deeper meanings and thoughts of people in ages past.

The early translators—the monks, the scribes and men of religion—knew in their inner beings that they had to see every word as sacred and translate every passage with extreme care, whether they understood its meaning or not. Because of their devotion and dedication, and a visionary King James, *The King James Version of the Holy Bible* is a book of the rarest quality.

In my search for truth, I had to sift through and examine carefully every word and every verse as if it were a fragile fossil in my hands. Like an archaeologist would to interpret the past, I had to *tune into the Bible*, for *its* ways are like the pictures we see in our dreams when we sleep. Sometimes they are in symbols and at times they are factual; sometimes there is a blending of the two. That is how it is with the Bible, and that is how I discovered the many waters.

> Give ear, O my people, to my law: incline your ears to the words of my mouth. I will open my mouth in a parable: I will utter dark sayings of old. Psalm 78:1 – 2

I
Alpha and Omega

In the beginning God created the heaven and the earth.
Genesis 1:1

"In the *beginning*. . . ."

THERE is no better way to start creation than at the very beginning. The word *begin* means to do the first part of an action, to come into being, and thus begins the concept of *Time*.

Many centuries ago, Maimonides, a physician, philosopher and codifier of the Jewish Talmud, wrote:

> God created everything out of nothing. Time is also a divine creation, since without a moving thing there cannot be motion, and without motion there is no time.[1]

We are made of matter, we live in a material world, and we have our being in linear time. There is motion and evolution, beginnings and endings; time and limits rule our lives.

> To every thing there is a season, and a time to every purpose under the heaven: A time to be born, and a time to die. . . .
>
> Ecclesiastes 3:1 – 2

In the first verse of Genesis, the *beginning* is the start of our time-period on earth. Stephen Hawking entitled his book *A Brief History of Time*, and that would also be an apt title for the biblical creation story. The cosmos had a beginning, and it will end, but Alpha and Omega always has been and always will be—forever.

We cannot fathom eternity. Time without beginning or end is a concept that our astronomers and physicists are grappling with now as they study the cosmos.

"In the beginning *God*. . . ."

God is neither male nor female, but before I continue I must emphasize that I will stay with convention and refer to God as *he*. Throughout the history of most of the people and nations that believe in God, the Supreme Being is a male, a Father image. This has always been the thought and practice in Judaism, the source of our Bible.

We tend to personify things by giving them a name and a gender. Ships come to mind as usually being female, and hurricanes were always female until some women objected. One universal personified female is Mother Earth, or Mother Nature. Thus we have God the Father, the giver of life, and Mother Earth, from whose body we come and are nurtured throughout our lives. All life is the child of God the Father and Mother Nature.

> For in him we live, and move, and have our being...For we are also his offspring. Acts 17:28

There has been more misunderstanding, dissension and confusion about God than any other entity in the world's history. *Who* is he? *Where* is he? *What* is he? Most people have an irrational and childlike concept of God, and so it comes as no surprise that we have atheists and people who argue whether God is a man or a woman. God is not a white-bearded old man sitting sternly on a golden throne, up there on a fluffy cloud. Nor is she a woman in a business suit, planning and directing the universe from her heavenly computer.

God is Energy. God is Light. God is the Energy of all energy and the Light of all light—The Main Powerhouse! He is Conscious Energy, the Soul of souls, the Mind of minds and all of our mental processes. He is the Life of all life. He is the source of all that exists.

We do not know what energy is. We know how to use some forces of energy, but we don't know how it originated or where it comes from. Energy is the all-embracing power of the universe, and it cannot be destroyed. It exists and there is no other explanation for it, a mystery that will never be resolved. Our cosmos is made of matter, all of it, but there can be no matter without energy for matter *is* a form of energy. That is *what* God is.

The highest intensity of energy is life and all other forms of energy exist only to accommodate life. Within the forces of life there is mind, consciousness and soul. These are one and the same, with many variations. All life, be it human, animal or plant has some form of mind. I am not referring to the brain. The brain is only the vehicle, the outer casing, in animal life, through which the mind functions while we are on earth. We don't think of plants and some lower species of animals as having a mind, but then we don't really know what mind is. Can anyone explain memory, or emotions, or feelings? These too are forces of energy, but we don't know what energy is.

Scientists will argue that the lower species of animal life exist only on instinct, but what is instinct? Could it be memory that is not of the brain, but from the cells or genes? We think of ourselves as the highest form of life (rightly so), and yet we still bring some instincts into the world with us at birth, such as the instinct to suck and grasp, and the ability to swim.

The highest, most profound properties of life are Mind, Consciousness and Soul. These are the essence of heaven and earth, and that is *who* God is.

> And God said to Moses, I AM THAT I AM.... Exodus 3:14

> Jesus said: "You have neither heard his voice at any time, nor seen his shape." John 5:37

> Have you not known? Have you not heard, that the everlasting God, the LORD, the Creator of the ends of the earth, faints not, neither is weary? Isaiah 40:28

Even if it were possible to be in the presence of God we could not survive the experience. Think of the one star that lights up our world and nourishes all life on this planet. We call it the sun. It is a rather insignificant star in one of millions of galaxies in the cosmos, but it is our world's most dynamic source of energy. Every second of every day, about four million tons of its mass is transformed into energy, yet only two billionths of this energy ever reaches our planet. But we need that small fraction, as all life depends on it either directly or indirectly. However, too much of a good thing can be harmful. Blindness can result from looking directly at the sun without protection, and radiation burns from too much exposure can cause cancer. The Energy and the Light that is God is so phenomenal that no one can approach him and live. We would become "crispy critters" in his presence.

> ...You cannot see my face: for there shall no man see me, and live.
>
> Exodus 33:20

God, the Creator of the sun and the cosmos, is eternal, immortal and invisible "...dwelling in the light which no man can approach; whom no man has seen, nor can see... ." (1 Timothy 6:16)

Throughout the Bible, the word *light* is used to describe the forces of energy. The people of the time could see the properties of light, but they were also aware that there were forces that they could not see and these they referred to as "the invisible." Light was also a symbol of spiritual awareness and knowledge, in contrast to darkness and ignorance.

As all life needs water, it too was a symbol of life—both physical life and spiritual life. All life *is* water and light.

> For with you is the fountain of life: in your light shall we see light.
>
> Psalm 36:9

God is not in a place because God *is* the place. God is around everything and is everything—no beginning, no ending and no boundary. That is *where* God is.

> One God and Father of all, who is above all, and through all, and in you all.
>
> Ephesians 4:6

In the Bible, there is frequent testimony from those who claim to have seen God or who spoke to him, and he with them. The Bible is full of *God said this* and *God said that.* Therefore, what I am saying may seem like a contradiction, but it isn't. God spoke then—and still does now—through the process of *Thought*! The contradiction lies in the ancient people's expression of their thoughts. Their perception of their God, and their understanding of nature and the world in which they lived can be very confusing to the modern reader.

> For, lo, he that formed the mountains, and created the wind, and declared to man what is his thought... . Amos 4:13

How does God declare his Thought?

> In the beginning was the Word, and the Word was with God, and the Word was God. The same was in the beginning with God. All things were made by him; and without him was not anything made that was made. In him was life; and the life was the light of men. And the light shines in darkness; and the darkness comprehended it not. John 1:1–5

The most pronounced Thought of God was the Word that came down through the generations in the physical form of stone, papyrus and scroll. The Word was written in stages and over time by men who were able to *hear* the Thought of God, but they were human nonetheless. They wrote with human hands and human hearts, and sometimes they had the tendency to make God in their own image. As they thought, so did their God. He had a temper and sometimes lost control of it. He held grudges and occasionally had someone murdered. He favored some people or some nations and punished others—or had them destroyed. He was a jealous God, and was almost always in a bad mood. It appears that, at times, some of these ancient writers had trouble separating their thoughts and feelings from spiritual insight.

> You shall not add to the word which I command you, neither shall you diminish anything from it, that you may keep the commandments of the LORD your God which I command you.
> Deuteronomy 4:2

> For my thoughts are not your thoughts, neither are your ways my ways...For as the heavens are higher than the earth, so are my ways higher than your ways, and my thoughts than your thoughts.
>
> Isaiah 55:8–9

> But God has revealed them to us by his Spirit: for the Spirit searches all things, yes, the deep things of God. 1 Corinthians 2:10

God is a Spirit (with an uppercase *S*). We are spirits (with a lower case *s*). We are spirits clothed in matter and a minute fraction of the Creator's beam of Light.

We were created to be gods. We are a restless and curious species, always searching and reaching for the "deep things" of the Spirit of God (whether we are aware of it or not). That is why we have philosophers, scholars, scientists and artists. That is why I wrote this book and that is why you are reading it. It is the God in us. That is how God *speaks* and reveals his Thought—from Spirit to spirit, from Mind to mind and from Soul to soul.

So, what about all those who claimed to have seen God and talked to him? Moses spent time with God on Mount Sinai and received, directly from him, the Ten Commandments written on tablets with God's own hands. How does one explain that?

Actually, none of those people ever saw God, spoke with him or he with them. Moses did not see God and God did not chisel the commandments into stone. Nor did they wine and dine together. Somebody gave Moses the Tablets to present to the people, but it wasn't God.

No one has ever seen God, no one has ever heard his voice, and no one can approach him and live. He is Light that is invisible to all life in heaven and on earth.

Who the patriarchs of those ancient times saw, heard and spoke to was the LORD God and the LORD. They had contact with the LORD God or the LORD via dreams, visions, meditation and prayer, and sometimes through mediums and oracles. All of the patriarchs of the Old Testament were prophets, psychics, and seers, well versed in the sciences of the day and the art of magic and astrology. Moses was said to be the greatest of them all. It was also said of Abraham that, when he still lived in the city of Ur, the kings and princes from afar would come to him to see what the future held for them in the stars.

In the Old Testament, there are Gods, gods, LORDS, Lords, and, oh yes, lords, and to make it more confusing the Old Testament sometimes refers to a LORD and a Lord in the same sentence. A Lord in the Old Testament is a man of this planet, and a LORD is from heaven or the heavens.

The New Testament does not use LORD (all uppercase); it is always written as Lord and it mostly refers to Jesus.

Before translations took place, the writers of the original Torah (Old Testament) texts made it very clear as to which Lord they were referring, but the syntax in every language is different and confusing, and the translators may have resorted to uppercase letters instead of names. This is one reason why some biblical texts have been misunderstood. Another notable misinterpretation throughout the Bible is where it states that people were in fear of God or were to fear God. The early Hebrew language had no word for religion so the translators, to explain a form of reverence and awe, used the word *fear*.

If we are to interpret the Bible correctly, we must recognize that God, the Supreme Being, the Creator, the Almighty, is above *all* titles and there are still verses that point out, quite clearly, that God is not a LORD or a Lord.

> The mighty God, even the LORD, has spoken.... Psalm 50:1

> Thus says the LORD, the Holy One of Israel, and his Maker....
> Isaiah 45:11

> ...the LORD the King of Israel, and his redeemer the LORD of hosts.... Isaiah 44:6

> Great is the LORD, and greatly to be praised in the city of our God, in the mountain of his holiness. Psalm 48:1

At this point in the text, it will suffice to say that these entities are not one and the same and I will elaborate when we get to heaven—the interpretation of the word *heaven*, that is.

"In the beginning God *created*... ."

To create means to bring something into existence by one's own thought and imagination.

The Mind of minds was not—and is not—a God of religion. It was humankind that thought up religion. God the Creator is a scientist, the original one. He is the source of all the sciences.

The cosmos took a great deal of thought, planning, and a vivid imagination. We can only marvel at the creativity of nature—the animate and the inanimate, and the starry night sky. From this main source of creativity we too are marvelous creations and we are gods that can think and plan and imagine the most phenomenal of concepts.

> For by him were all things created, that are in heaven, and that are in earth, visible and invisible, whether they be thrones, or dominions, or principalities, or powers: all things were created by him, and for him:
> Colossians 1:16

> All these things you did establish in your wisdom. You did appoint all your works before ever creating them.
> (*The Dead Sea Scrolls: The Hymns*)[2]

Creativity is basically an instinctive drive for perfection, and it is in every living plant and animal. It is that constant need, conscious or unconscious, throughout the eons of time to change form, to adapt, or to change course and strive for improvement. It is called *evolution*.

Evolution is a creative, God-given process, and creativity requires thought.

God created the process of evolution as the main physical law of the cosmos. God did not create energy and its many forces of light—God *is* Light. God did not create life—God *is* Life. He just extended his Energy and his Life into what was to become the heaven and the earth, and with the power of his thought, through the laws of evolution, he said, "Let there be…and there was…and let it bring forth…and it brought forth."

Every living plant and creature has in it that mysterious instinct to survive and to recreate itself into perfection. What makes a certain plant, over the millennia, *decide* that it will start eating the bug that lands on it? What makes a cute little succulent *decide* that it is going to grow round, lay low and resemble a pebble in the sand? What makes an insect, over the course of time, change to look like a dry twig on a tree, or like a leaf fluttering in the breeze? For that matter, why does the dandelion in the lawn hug the ground so the lawnmower blades can't reach it while the one in the flowerbed strives to reach the sky? Behind all of creation, and all that exists, there is thought.

Humans, and other animals, think through physical brains, and thinking is a vibration. When we think—and we think all of the time, day and night, because energy does not rest—our brains produce electrical impulses known as *brain waves*. These waves, in turn, produce cycles called *alpha, beta, theta, and delta*: from wide-awake, or outer consciousness, to a deep sleep.

While in the alpha state, we can become one with our inner self (spirit). Alpha is the state conducive to relaxation, peacefulness, gaining knowledge and wisdom, and especially for prayer and meditation. In other words, it promotes creative thought and that is the God in us.

Before I close on the subject of creativity, I would like to introduce an exercise that I learned many years ago. This exercise helped me realize just how powerful thought can be.

Choose a nice sunny day, but with a few fluffy white clouds in the sky. Find a quiet, comfortable spot to sit or lie where you have a good view of the sky. Choose a cloud. It should be a large cloud that does not appear to be moving. Now concentrate on that cloud. At that moment, it is *your* cloud; you become one with that cloud. Keep your eyes on it and concentrate! Then with your eyes, slice it down the middle. Keep slicing—and stay calm. As you slice with your eyes and your mind, the cloud will separate down the middle. It might take awhile on your first try, but eventually you will gain confidence. Then in a minute or two you can go around slicing clouds.

Try more! Pick another cloud and bore a hole in it—right through the middle. You can do it! You can shape the cloud any way you wish. When you become really good at this exercise, choose a spot in the sky that has no clouds and in the clear blue emptiness envision a cloud. Keep your image strong and don't let go of it. A cloud will begin to materialize. Then, picture in your mind that the cloud *be gone*. It will not move to the right or the left; it will just evaporate.

What you are dealing with is only vapor and dust, but think of how far away it is in physical terms. Thought has no boundaries. The mind knows no time or distance. This is the God in you.

"In the beginning God created the *heaven*. . . ."

Let us briefly recap the *beginning* to understand more clearly the creation of heaven.

In the first verse in the first book of the Bible, creation had not yet begun. It is a statement that presents the fact that in the beginning of time, as we know it, there was God and only God. There was nothing else (if one can imagine that), and there is no better place for a profound statement than in the first verse of the Word of God.

Accurately speaking, there was never a beginning—just a *breath*, but for the sake of the human mind, which cannot grasp the concept of *forever*, there has to be a beginning and a point in *Time*. When that time was cannot be calculated and is beyond human comprehension.

> I am Alpha and Omega, the beginning and the ending, says the Lord, which is, and which was, and which is to come, the Almighty.
>
> Revelation 1:8

To assist in the understanding of the following concepts see Figure 1 on the following page.

The third heaven, or the heaven of heavens, *always was*. It is the central sphere of the Light from which all things were created, and that is God. The Bible refers to it as the *throne of God*.

"The depth" or "the deep" mentioned in the Bible is the universe; the Bible also refers to this as *the sea*. It too *always was*, as it is situated within the central sphere of heaven and is the deepest, darkest and coldest part of God. It is *our* space.

What was created in these two areas is that which accommodates life and gives it meaning: celestial life in the third heaven and terrestrial life in the second heaven, or the heavens.

Not many of the creation stories from ancient civilizations around the world start at the very beginning, as does the King James Version of the Bible. Not even *The Revised English Bible* has the creation account completely correct. It states, "In the beginning God created the heavens and the earth." One little *s* at the end of heaven makes a big difference—it changes the entire meaning of the Word of God, and this is when misinterpretation begins.

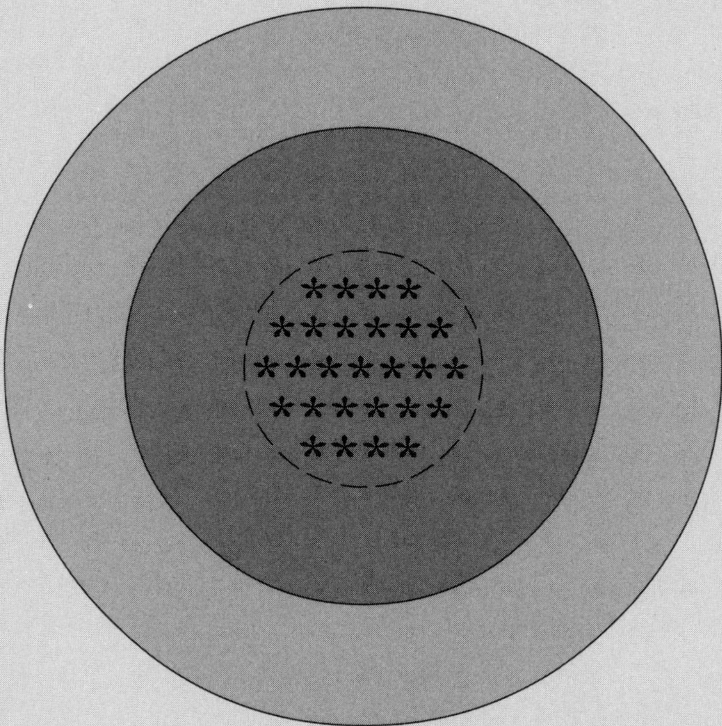

God: Energy, Light. There is no Time. There is no distance. It is Forever.

Heaven: the third heaven, the heaven of heavens, God's throne, paradise.

The heavens: the second heaven, the deep, the universe.

** **Earth**: matter, the expanding cosmos, the many waters, (the atmosphere surrounding each of the many waters is not shown; this atmosphere is the first heaven, the one that gives us breath and rain).

Throughout the King James Bible, the third heaven (the heaven of heavens) is always in the singular (with no *s*). It is truly the heaven of heavens and it was this celestial heaven that was established and populated first.

> I knew a man in Christ... (whether in the body...or whether out of the body)...caught up to the third heaven...caught up into paradise.... 2 Corinthians 12:2–4

> Behold, the heaven and the heaven of heavens is the LORD'S....
> Deuteronomy 10:14

> ...behold, the heaven and the heaven of heavens cannot contain you.... 1 Kings 8:27

The first heaven, like the third heaven, is in the singular, but is easily distinguished from the third heaven by the verse describing it. It is the atmosphere that surrounds our planet and gives us breath, clouds, and rain.

> And it came to pass...that the heaven was black with clouds and wind, and there was a great rain.... 1 Kings 18:45

Now, let's get back to the (celestial) heaven.

> For by him were all things created, that are in heaven...visible and invisible...thrones...dominions...principalities...powers....
> Colossians 1:16

This region is real, as real as the universe. It is a *place*. Its principalities and dominions, thrones and powers, are populated with beings that are not made of matter, but rather a force of energy known as *spirit*.

Spirit is the personality of life, and all life has spirit. On earth we are spirits clothed in matter, and heavenly beings are spirits clothed in light.

These heavenly entities are the LORDS (New Testament—Lords), the archangels, and their angelic hosts of helpers, angels, and seraphim. They were created for one purpose only and that is to serve the Light that is God, who has no shape or form, and cannot be seen or heard.

The LORDS are the embodiment of God in the third heaven. They were created and ordained to be intermediaries between God and humankind and they have the power and authority to speak and act in the name of God. In essence they are God, but they are below God. They are what we would today call the LORDS *of* God and the names of these LORDS are seldom mentioned in the Bible because they speak for God and not of themselves.

The Hebrew tribes had a LORD God (a LORD *of* God) who looked after them and who guided them personally. His name was *Jehovah*. Jehovah was not just another name for God as is believed by biblical scholars. He was the LORD of this planet for the first Homo sapiens, and later for the Israelites, the ancestors of Jesus.

The archangels and their hosts of angels are the messengers and helpers of the LORDS of God. We cannot see them either, because they are of a higher vibration of energy than we are, and matter is the lowest of vibrations. Occasionally, however, under the right conditions of atmosphere or whatever it takes, an angel can be seen, and it is not a figment of the imagination. Our world still has a lot to learn about energy and light.

Although we as humans are clothed in matter, we too have our eternal *home*—just like the invisibles of heaven. When we die—so called—and drop our *earthly garments*, our worn out, diseased or battered *clothing* will return to the dust from which it came, and we will *return* to the heaven of heavens and to one of the principalities known as *paradise*. While we are there we are *as* the angels and all the hosts of heaven. We will not *be* angels, as people like to think. We are "lower than the angels." Nor will we be in the presence of God. God's power and radiant light is above and beyond the third heaven, and the invisibles do not see him or have contact with him either as they too would be destroyed in his presence.

The Bible refers to heaven as *God's throne*, but he is above the heaven of heavens—above and around it.

> Is not God in the height of heaven? and behold the height of the stars, how high they are...and he walks in the circuit of heaven.
>
> Job 22:12–14

According to the Bible, the Son of God was the first of all beings and is the highest entity in heaven. He was, and is, the Son (uppercase *S*). He is the

LORD of all LORDS and of all the hosts of heaven and is the highest being next to God. His name is *Jesus*.

Throughout the Scriptures, in both the Old and the New Testaments, there is a distinction between the Son of God and the sons of God. Please take note of this, as it is very, very important in order to interpret the Bible correctly.

All humans on this planet, and throughout the universe, are the sons of God because we were created in the "image" of God.

This is only one of the errors that have been overlooked, or ignored, by scholars and readers alike, and as a result there is a misinterpretation. In Genesis 6:2 when the "sons of God saw the daughters of men that they were fair. . . ." people have assumed that angels came down from heaven and married human women. No. Angels do not mix with humans. They do not have physical bodies, and were created only to serve God and be messengers for the LORDS of God. I will elaborate on this most interesting subject in Chapter Nine: Giants and Men of Renown.

> Whereas angels, which are greater in power and might. . . .
> 2 Peter 2:11

> Man. . .a little lower than the angels. . . . Hebrews 2:7

> For he shall give his angels charge over you, to keep you in all your ways. Psalm 91:11

> Are they not all ministering spirits, sent forth to minister for them who shall be heirs of salvation? Hebrews 1:14

The Son of God, the Lord of Lords, was also called the *Son of man*. This means that not only is he the highest being next to God the Energy and the Light, but he was also given the properties of humankind. He was made to "sit on the right hand side of God," but could also walk down a dusty road with men who are made of clay. No one else in the invisible world can do that. Like all of us in heaven and on earth, he cannot see God either or have personal contact, but he is God, clothed in Light in the third heaven, and clothed in matter when he was on our planet two thousand years ago.

There is God the Father—the Light of heaven and earth who is above all, around all, and in all. There is God the Son—the Son of God and Son of man. There is God the Holy Ghost (Spirit), and we have in us the Spirit of God—the life and personality that is God.

God the Father, God the Son, and God the Holy Spirit!

Rabbi Solomon ben Isaac, also known as Rashi, born in 1040, was a prominent commentator of the Talmud. In one of his writings he explained the phrase in Deuteronomy, "Hear, O Israel, The LORD our God, the Lord is One." This means that the LORD of Israel would one day not just be the God of the Jews, but would be the ONE SOLE GOD of the world, as it is written in Zechariah 14:9, "In that day shall the Lord our God be One and His name One."[3] He was referring to the Saviour and Redeemer that the Jewish nation has been waiting for. That would be the LORD of LORDS, the "only begotten Son of God," JESUS, whom they do not accept or recognize.

> For God so loved the world, that he gave his only begotten Son. . . .
> John 3:16

> No man has seen God at any time; the only begotten Son, which is in the bosom of the Father, he has declared him. John 1:18

> But to which of the angels said he at any time, Sit on my right hand, until I make your enemies your footstool? Hebrews 1:13

The *6th and 7th Books of Moses*[4] are manuscripts, supposedly written by Moses that were not included in the canon because they were considered witchcraft by the early churches. Moses grew up in the king's palace and would have learned the magic that Egypt was well known for at the time. The contents in these books are a mystery to the modern reader, and I agree that they would not have made good canon material for our present day Bible; however, there are some interesting bits of information that can add to our knowledge of the Bible.

These writings make it quite clear to the reader that Lord and God are not the same entity, and it names the Lords and archangels who are appointed to *look after* this world. Some of these names can also be found in the Bible, but scholars have mistaken them for the names of God. The names of some of the Lords are *Adonai, Sother, Emmanuel, Ehie, Tetragramaton, Atscher, Jehovah,* and *Sabaoth—the Good*, also known as *the Lord of light*. A host of Lords was known as the *Elohem*. Jehovah was the Lord of the Israelites during their exile from Egypt, and was even mentioned in the creation story as the Lord who instigated the creation of Adam and Eve.

> Hear the voice of your God through me, Jehovah, Aglai, the God of heaven and earth. . . .[5]

These writings also give the names of angels and archangels. The names of the angels would be too numerous to mention here, and of little interest to us unless we got to know them personally of course, but some of the archangels are well known to Bible readers. They are Michael, Gabriel, Raphael, Uriel and Thronus.

> Yea, while I was speaking in prayer, even a man Gabriel, whom I had seen in the vision at the beginning, being caused to fly swiftly, touched me. . . . Daniel 9:21

> And, behold, one like the similitude of the sons of men touched my lips...Then there came again and touched me one like the appearance of a man...and there is none that holds with me in these things, but Michael your prince. Daniel 10:16–21

> And the angel said to him [Zacharias], I am Gabriel, that stand in the presence of God; and am sent to speak to you. . . . Luke 1:19

The seraphim are entities of the third heaven. *The 6th and 7th Books of Moses* mention them right along with the other hosts of heaven, but nothing is said about who they are, or what they are. I read an article that stated they are the highest entities in heaven. That's not likely. The Son of God is the highest, then the LORDS (Lords), and then the archangels and their hosts of angels. The books of Moses also mention helpers and servants along with the seraphim.

The seraphim, according to the Bible, had six wings and appeared to be more like a very intelligent creature than an angel, while angels have been described in the Bible as having human form. And no, angels do not have wings. When the Bible speaks of them "flying swiftly" it means that they would appear and disappear swiftly, and the writers of the time did not have a better way of describing this. Artists in the Middle Ages took this biblical description literally and painted wings on angels, and that is why we have angels with wings today.

> In the year that king Uzziah died I also saw the Lord sitting upon a throne, high and lifted up, and his train filled the temple. Above it stood the seraphims: each one had six wings; with two he covered his face, and with two he covered his feet, and with two he did fly. And one called to another, and said, Holy, holy, holy, is the LORD of hosts: the whole earth is full of his glory…Then flew one of the seraphims unto me, having a live coal in his hand, which he had taken with the tongs from off the altar… . Isaiah 6:1–6

What this particular verse tells us is that the seraphim may not have been members of the heavenly host at all. They were earthly beings of some kind. Isaiah saw "the Lord sitting upon the throne…and his train filled the temple."

In the Old Testament, Lord (with only the *L* uppercase) was a man of this planet and not a LORD of heaven. His temple was an earthly building and the seraphim stood above his throne. They called one to another and praised the LORD of hosts (the one in heaven). Then a seraphim flew to Isaiah, "having a live coal in his hand which he had taken with tongs from off the altar." A live coal is an earthly object, and an angelic spirit would not have needed tongs to pick up the hot coal.

The seraphim remain somewhat obscure and perhaps mysterious. Readers will have to draw their own conclusions.

Then there are the cherubims. This will come as a bit of a surprise to readers of the Bible and other religious literature who have always assumed that these too were angels of some kind. To the general public, a cherub is the cute little baby angel called cupid who flies around with a bow and arrow and aims at those who are to fall in love. How that originated I will never know, but neither the angel of lower order nor the cherub with the bow and arrow are anywhere near the facts presented in the Bible or *The Dead Sea Scrolls.*

The first mention of cherubims is in Genesis 3:24, when Adam and Eve were removed from the garden of Eden, and a flaming sword and Cherubims (in this case the word *cherubims* was capitalized) were placed at the entrance. In this account the Cherubims were not sent there to stand guard, as angels would have been. They were placed into position, along with the flaming sword.

In Exodus 25:19–22, the LORD gives Moses instructions on making a sanctuary and a place for the safekeeping of the testimony that he will give them. To be included with the elaborate details on the building process were the cherubims.

> And make one cherub on the one end, and the other cherub on the other end: even of the mercy seat shall you make the cherubims on the two ends thereof. And the cherubims shall stretch forth their wings on high, covering the mercy seat with their wings…And you shall put the mercy seat above upon the ark; and in the ark you shall put the testimony that I shall give you. And there I will meet with you, and I will commune with you from above the mercy seat, from between the two cherubims… .

There were to be two cherubims, one on each side of the mercy seat. Their wings were to cover the mercy seat, and the mercy seat had to be between the cherubims and nowhere else. Could the "wings" perhaps have been antennas to pick up signals?

Unlike most accounts in the Bible where the patriarchs and prophets spoke to the LORD via dreams and visions, this was no dream or vision. Moses was given specific instructions and told exactly where, and how, to install a *communication system* so that the LORD could communicate with them. When it was all completed according to the plan "Moses…heard the voice of one speaking to him from off the mercy seat that was upon the ark of testimony, from between the two cherubims: and he spoke to him." (Numbers 7:89)

As we know from the Old Testament, a LORD was from heaven, but the scribes did not distinguish between a LORD from heaven and a LORD from "the heavens," who would have been someone from another planet. In the Old Testament, only Lords were from our world. Because the Old Testament uses all uppercase letters for a LORD from heaven and a LORD from the heavens, we can only differentiate the two by the content of the passage.

Again, the New Testament and all other religious literature use "Lord."

The LORD that gave Moses the instructions on how to build the sanctuary so that he could communicate with him was not from the heaven of heavens. Those LORDS do not need a system made with instruments because they communicate via thought, dreams and visions. Who then was this LORD?

> Give ear, O Shepherd of Israel, you who led Joseph like a flock; you who dwell between the cherubims, shine forth. Psalm 80:1

To shine forth? To shine is energy that is light. Was David, in his psalms, pleading with the LORD that once led his people as a shepherd would a flock, to give them a call through an instrument of some kind? This particular LORD was no longer in communication with these people, and David felt that he was still needed.

Four hundred and eighty years after the children of Israel had left Egypt, and in the fourth year of Solomon's reign over Israel, Solomon built a huge and elaborate "house of the LORD." In this building was placed an oracle, which is a special sanctuary for communication with the deity. The oracle was covered with cedar and pure gold, as was "the whole house." Within the oracle he made:

> ...two cherubims of olive tree, each ten cubits high [approximately 15 feet]...and he set the cherubims within the inner house, and they stretched forth the wings of the cherubims so that the wing of one touched the one wall, and the wing of the other touched the other wall, and their wings touched one another in the midst of the house...and he overlaid the cherubims with gold...and he carved all the walls of the house round about with carved figures of cherubims and palm trees and open flowers. 1 Kings 6:22–29

Solomon placed his cherubims exactly as Moses had done except that his were much larger. This whole building was set up for a communication system, and a place for worship of their LORD from the sky. But just imagine this building! One would have to read the entire chapter of this text to get the full impact of its beauty and extravagance.

It also mentions that Solomon had all the walls carved with palm trees, open flowers and figures of cherubims.

Carved cherubims in the scenes of palm trees and open flowers?

People like Moses, Solomon and David were educated, as were most patriarchs, princes and kings in that time, and knew some of the mysteries and the magic of the universe that our world has forgotten over the millennia. Ordinary people of the biblical era were not educated; in fact most could not even read or write. Any mysterious phenomenon that they happened to see in the sky or on land was attributed to "the glory of God," the "LORD God" or his angels.

Ezekiel tells of a vision in which he saw the glory of the God of Israel and the glory of the LORD was gone up from the cherub that he was on:

> Then I looked, and, behold in the firmament that was above the head of the cherubims...And he spoke with the man clothed in linen, and said, Go in between the wheels, even under the cherub, and fill your hands with coals of fire from between the cherubims...Now the cherubims stood on the right side of the house, when the man went in; and the cloud filled the inner court. Then the glory of the LORD went up from the cherub...and the house was filled with the cloud, and the court was full of the brightness of the LORD'S glory. And the sound of the cherubim's wings was heard...as the voice of the Almighty God when he speaks. And there appeared in the cherubims the form of a man's hand under their wings...behold the four wheels by the cherubims...and the four had one likeness, as if a wheel had been in the midst of a wheel...they turned not as they went. And their whole body...and the wheels, were full of eyes round about...And the cherubims lifted up...and when the cherubims lifted up their wings to mount up from the earth, the same wheels also turned not from beside them...for the spirit of the living creature was in them. Then the glory of the LORD departed from off the threshold of the house, and stood over the cherubims. This is the living creature that I saw under the God of Israel...and the likeness of the hands of a man was under their wings.... Ezekiel 10:1 – 21

One can only imagine Ezekiel's astonishment at seeing this creature and its strange behavior. All those eyes round about, and the man's hands under the wings must have been a real mystery. Nor did the coals of fire under this animal help to solve the mystery, but to us it provides enough evidence that this was a machine, not an animal.

Ezekiel thought that he had seen a vision, but it may have been an actual event. He would assume it to be a vision because he knew that there was no such living creature, and it would have to be symbolic. He was a priest and he knew that the LORD God of heaven was a spirit and did not just pop in on mere mortals. It was all too preposterous to be real.

It was mentioned that Solomon had all the walls of the house carved with palm trees, open flowers and figures of cherubims. These cherubim figures on the walls may not have been a replica of those that graced the oracle. It appears that the word *cherubim* may have been used to describe a communication instrument *and* to describe an electronically based sky ship. The reason would be that both used the properties of light that shone forth, and both had a connection to another planet. Neither of these cherubims was an angel.

The Divine Throne-Chariot

The following fragment was found in Qumran along with the discovery of the Dead Sea Scrolls believed to be from the sect known as the Essenes. J. Strugnell made this particular translation in 1960, under the title *The Angelic Liturgy at Qumran*. The words in parentheses are assumed to be what was intended, as the manuscript was in very poor condition.

> ...the [ministers] of the Glorious Face in the abode of [the gods] of knowledge fall down before Him, [and the cherubim] utter blessings. And as they rise up, there is a divine small voice...and loud praise; (there is) a divine [small] voice as they fold their wings.
>
> The cherubim bless the image of the Throne-Chariot above the firmament, and they praise the [majesty] of the fiery firmament beneath the seat of His Glory. And beneath the turning wheels, Angels of Holiness come and go, as it were a fiery vision of most

> holy spirits; and about them (flow) seeming rivulets of fire, like gleaming bronze, a radiance of many gorgeous colors, of marvellous pigments magnificently mingled.
>
> The spirits of the living God move perpetually with the glory of the wonderful Chariot. The small voice of blessing accompanies the tumult as they depart, and on the path of their return they worship the Holy One. Ascending, they rise marvellously; settling, they [stay] still. The sound of joyful praise is silenced and there is a small voice of blessing in all the camp of God. And the voice of praise [resounds] from the midst of all their divisions in [worship of]...and each one in his place, all their numbered ones sing hymns of praise.[6]

Scholars think that the writers of this text got their inspiration from the book of Ezekiel and their imaginations took over from there. I don't think so. Men like Moses, David and Solomon were well acquainted with cherubims. In their accounts there was no hint of surprise or mystery, nor was there a sense of worship toward the cherubim. Ezekiel, on the other hand, was a priest in bondage at the time of his experience and probably not educated in the worldly sciences of the time. To Ezekiel, what he saw was a creature, and the LORD rode on this live animal of unknown origin.

What the writers of the Qumran text describe is a chariot that, supposedly, came from heaven and was driven by angels. Obviously these people were familiar with chariots, but because these were exceptionally beautiful they may have thought they were heavenly and the occupants angels. Who else could they be?

In the era of the Qumran scrolls, the Divine Throne-Chariot was also known as the *Merkabah*, and over time they would become objects of worship. To the Jewish people they were referred to as *Angelic cherubims*, and the Rabbinic Orthodoxy eventually felt that they had to step in and discourage the practice.

In some Jewish literature, such as the *Mishnah*, Ezekiel's chapter of his vision is forbidden to the common man. It even lays down the law that "no wise man is to share his understanding of the Merkabah with a person less enlightened than himself."[7] That pretty well took care of the subject, and so far no other written material on the Divine Throne-Chariot, the Merkabah, or the Angelic cherubim have been found.

"No wise man is to share his understanding of the Merkabah with a person less enlightened than himself."

A very significant statement! What it says is the wise men of the day knew all about the Merkabah and who the so-called angels actually were. The general public, however, was not aware of them, and any knowledge given out in a haphazard way would only cause confusion and maybe even fear to the uninitiated.

Sounds familiar.

In India, there are Sanskrit texts several thousand years old that, in amongst all of their fascinating legends and mythology, contain accounts of flying ships that "go on their own force like a bird, on earth, on water, or in air." These "Vimana" can fly through the skies and can visit other planets. Some of these stories even give descriptions of the building process, which have drawn modern day scientists to the ancient writings.[8]

Whether the vehicles were known as *Vimana, Throne-Chariots, Merkabahs* or *cherubims*, they were of the earth and piloted by earthly beings. Angels are spirits that "fly swiftly" and can appear and disappear whenever and wherever they want; they do not need to race around in the skies in motorized machines.

I have included the cherubims in the topic of heaven because they have always been associated with the heavenly host. I find it amazing that the true identity has never been recognized, or has it been that no one has wanted to see it? That is all too common in our society. There are many pebbles and shells of truth in the sands that some people would rather not see, or have to deal with.

Now that the cherubims have been grounded and removed from heavenly status, I will continue with those who really are *up there*.

The Bible doesn't provide much detail on the heavenly beings that were created before we were (how they live or what they may look like) and that oversight may have been intentional by the Christian church. The same authors that are in the canon certainly had enough information from among the ancient writings and manuscripts.

As I've mentioned before, the hosts of heaven are invisible to us. They are closer to the Light, so they are of a much higher vibration than we who dwell in the depth of God.

The *Pistis Sophia*[9] contains the fragmented gospels that have survived from an ancient Gnostic Bible that was called *The Books of the Saviour* and dates approximately 200 AD. These gospels claim to have preserved the secret mysteries of the worlds of the invisibles, as Jesus taught his initiates after the crucifixion and before his ascension into heaven.

Jesus, the Son of God, the Lord of Lords, was of the host of heaven and was an invisible before he entered this planet to teach us the true and natural way to live as sons of God rather than sons of men. We would have to assume that he would appear only to his disciples after the resurrection and would be invisible to everyone else because before his death these initiates had already been conditioned in spiritual knowledge and wisdom.

The religion of Gnosticism became a real challenge for Christianity and a serious rival for Jewish Orthodoxy. It delved into the mysteries of the invisible principalities and powers within the heaven of heavens, and their books were in poetic allegory and symbolism. There were the entities and the beings of heaven and, among them, the various energies of emotion and thoughts were personified, which probably made it rather confusing to a reader. Thus, there is wisdom personified as a woman named *Sophia*, from which one of the manuscripts gets its title: *Pistis Sophia; the faith of Sophia.*

The Books of the Saviour were eventually suppressed when the Roman Catholic Church gained control of Christianity, and lost to many generations was the beauty and mysticism that they contained. Like the Bible, they too have their share of sand to be sifted through, but on these ancient shores of literature even the sand is a challenge.

Some of the quotations in these writings are of great value in understanding the realm of energy and the properties of light, as Jesus explained it to his initiates.

> Jesus said to James: "...I say to you, You shall be the first in the kingdom of heaven before all the invisibles, and all the gods and rulers who are in the thirteenth aeon and in the twelfth aeon; and not only you, but also everyone who shall accomplish my mysteries."
>
> Mary started forward again and said: "Yea, O Lord, this is what you did say to us one time before, 'The last shall be first, and the first shall be last.' The first then, who were created before us are the invisibles, for indeed they arose before mankind, they and the gods and the rulers; and the men who shall receive mysteries, will be the first in the kingdom of heaven."
>
> Jesus said to her: "Well said, Mary."[10]

And Mary said to Jesus: "...My Lord and Savior, of what manner then are the...invisibles and of what type, or rather of what quality are they, or of what quality is their light?"

And Jesus answered and said to Mary: "What is there in this world which is like unto them, or rather what region is there in this world which is comparable to them? Now, therefore, to what am I to liken them, or rather what am I to say concerning them? For nothing exists in this world to which I shall be able to liken them, and no form exists in it which is able to be like them...And no light exists in this world which is more excellent than the sun...The invisibles shine ten thousand times more than the light of the sun which is in this world...For the light of the sun in its shape in truth is not of this world, for its light pierces through many veils and regions...the region of the Virgin of Light, (God) shines ten thousand times more than the invisibles...And if I lead you into the region of the rulers of the Fate, then you will see the glory in which they are, and because of their overtowering great glory you will deem this world before you as the darkness of darknesses, and you look at the whole world of men, how it will have the condition of a speck of dust for you because of the great distance it is... ."[11]

All flesh is not the same flesh...There are also celestial bodies, and bodies terrestrial: but the glory of the celestial is one, and the glory of the terrestrial is another. 1 Corinthians 15:39–40

You, O God, have created the expanse of the heavens, and the host of heavenly lights, and the tasks of the spirits and the dominion of the Holy Ones... . (*The Dead Sea Scrolls: The War Rule*)[12]

As the host of heaven cannot be numbered, neither the sand of the sea measured... . Jeremiah 33:22

"In the beginning God created the heaven and the *earth*."

In the fifth century BC, an ancient historian named Thucydides confidently noted that nothing of importance had happened before his time.

> Where were you when I laid the foundations of the earth? Declare, if you have understanding. Job 38:4

Thucydides was a narcissistic myopic, but our planet has suffered somewhat from the same affliction. Somewhere back in time, we came to the conclusion that we, on this tiny planet, are all alone in this fantastically, overwhelmingly large universe, and, therefore, we must be very special. God made only us. *We* are an only child.

Maybe it's time we shed our egos and broadened our horizons. We call our galaxy *The Milky Way*, and we have named the planets in our solar system after ancient gods; even their moons have names, but what do we call our planet? *Earth*. That's it—Earth. We have earth all to ourselves. Perhaps we should have our planet, and our moon, legalized within the nations of the universe by giving them each a name because you see...

WE ARE NOT ALONE—AND WE ARE NOT ON EARTH.
WE ARE ONLY A MICROSCOPIC SPECK OF DUST *OF* THE EARTH.

> Jesus said to his disciples: "...if you go to where the invisibles are...and look back at the world of men...it will have the condition of a speck of dust because of the distance... ."[13]

We would not have to leave the universe for that observation. Just wandering around in the cosmos would have the same effect.

In the beginning when God created the earth, he extended his Energy down into what would become heaven and then further down into what the Bible refers to as *the deep* or *the depth* and what we call *the universe*.

(The biblical "deep" or "depth" was also used to describe the oceans and the internal planetary waters on occasion, but the verses pertaining to either subject are easy to distinguish by their content).

In this depth, God created a form and force of energy that the Bible refers to as *earth* and what we call *matter*.

Today we have named all matter that is within the universe *the cosmos*, and this matter, or earth, is energy in the form of solids, liquids and gases. Earth is actually only dust, and our planet is only a tiny speck of dust of the earth that in the beginning God created.

Words like *cosmos* and *universe* were not in the biblical translator's vocabulary and this is one of the reasons for the many misinterpretations throughout the Bible—especially the creation story.

Genesis 1:1 says that God created the earth. To readers of the Bible it has always been assumed that this meant our tiny planet because we have always called it *earth*. Think for a moment, how—and why—would our planet have been created before the rest of the cosmos?

In Proverbs 8:22–27, Wisdom personified as female said:

> The LORD possessed me in the beginning of his way, before his works of old. I was set up from everlasting, from the beginning, or ever the earth was. While as yet he had not made the earth...nor the highest part of the dust of the world. When he prepared the heavens, I was there: when he set a compass upon the face of the depth... .

"...he set a compass upon the face of the depth... ." The dictionary meaning of the word *deep* or *depth* is that which is the most central part; low in pitch; dark in color; intense; extreme. That describes the universe, or space, perfectly.

The black, cold vacuum that the stars, the planets, the galaxies and all other matter in the universe orbit, spin, spiral, or tumble around in was NOT created.

Actually, the word *vacuum* may not be the correct description of space. Some scientists have discovered that space may not be as empty as previously thought, and they are theorizing that a form of energy they call anti-gravity appears to be pulling the cosmos apart.

Steven Hawking once said, "The universe is neither created nor destroyed. It just is." He is right. The depth always was, and a "compass" was used to measure out the size of the cosmos to be and to set a limit as to how far it would expand within the universe. The universe has a boundary. It is a SPHERE in the center of the Light, and the heaven of heavens surrounds it.

> ...and he walks in the circuit of heaven... . Job 22:14

> I am Alpha and Omega, the beginning and the ending, says the Lord, which is, and which was, and which is to come, the Almighty.
> Revelation 1:8

"I am Alpha and Omega. . . ." Something that is both a beginning and an ending is a CIRCLE that goes around and around—forever.

The universe has a boundary and the third heaven has a boundary, but with God there are no limits. Can anyone imagine that? Can anyone imagine a space or an area that has no borders, which goes on in every direction—forever? With God there is no time and no distance. Alpha and Omega.

The *edge* of the universe may never be attainable by humankind. It is a sphere that has a barrier of light called a *firmament* that separates it from the heaven of the invisibles, and we can only leave our universe when we shed our earthly bodies and become one with the Light of lights.

> He stretches out the north over the empty place, and hangs the earth upon nothing. Job 26:7

> Have you perceived the breadth of the earth? Declare if you know it all. Job 38:18

> And, you, Lord, in the beginning have laid the foundation of the earth; and the heavens are the works of your hands: Hebrews 1:10

> I am the LORD that makes all things; that stretches forth the heavens alone: that spreads abroad the earth by myself; Isaiah 44:24

> The heavens declare the glory of God; and the firmament shows his handywork. Psalm 19:1

> Bless the LORD . . . Who covers yourself with light as with a garment: who stretches out the heavens like a curtain. . . . Psalm 104:2

Science has come to accept that the creation of matter within the universe started out with a "Big Bang" and we also know that the matter that was created with this big bang has been expanding for eons.

The universe does not expand. It's the matter (the cosmos) within the universe that has been expanding. We tend to use the two words interchangeably, but there is a distinction between the two in the Bible.

At a certain point in time—when this matter has reached the boundary of the universe—it will begin to contract, and it will do so for many more eons, until it is back to zero—and nothingness.

The expansion and contraction of the cosmos is just one breath of God, and only one brief history of time. Then, in another beginning, God will create the heaven and earth AGAIN!

Alpha and Omega—FOREVER

NOTES

1 Gersh, H. (1968). *The Sacred Books of the Jews*. New York, NY: Stein and Day Publishers., p. 194.

2 Vermes, G. (1962). *The Dead Sea Scrolls in English*. Middlesex, UK: Penguin., p. 191.

3 Gersh, H. (1968). *The Sacred Books of the Jews*. New York, NY: Stein and Day Publishers., p. 159–160.

4 *The Complete Edition of the 6th and7th Books of Moses*, Published for the trade: USA. "For the good of mankind." Translated from the Ancient Hebrew.

5 *The Complete Edition of the 6th and 7th Books of Moses*, Published for the trade: USA. "For the good of mankind." Translated from the Ancient Hebrew.

6 Vermes, G. (1962). *The Dead Sea Scrolls in English*. Middlesex, UK: Penguin., p. 212–213.

7 Vermes, G. (1962). *The Dead Sea Scrolls in English*. Middlesex, UK: Penguin., p. 211.

8 Drake, W.R. (1968). *Gods and Spacemen in the Ancient East*. Scarborough, ON: New American Library of Canada., p. 62.

9 Mead, G.R.S. (1974). *Pistis Sophia*. Secaucus, New Jersey: University Books Inc.

10 Mead, G.R.S. (1974). *Pistis Sophia*. Secaucus, New Jersey: University Books Inc., p. 81.

11 Mead, G.R.S. (1974). *Pistis Sophia*. Secaucus, New Jersey: University Books Inc., p. 155–156.

12 Vermes, G. (1962). *The Dead Sea Scrolls in English*. Middlesex, UK: Penguin., p. 137.

13 Mead, G.R.S. (1974). *Pistis Sophia*. Secaucus, New Jersey: University Books Inc., p. 156.

2
"Six Days"

And the earth was without form, and void; and darkness was upon the face of the deep. And the Spirit of God moved upon the face of the waters.
And God said, Let there be light: and there was light.
And God saw the light, that it was good: and God divided the light from the darkness.
And God called the light Day, and the darkness he called Night. And the evening and the morning were the first day.

Genesis 1:2 – 5

The First Day

"And the earth was without form, and void; and darkness was upon the face of the deep."

JUST as the first verse in the King James Bible was an all-inclusive statement that *God* created the heaven and the earth, the second verse states clearly that, as yet, there was no earth formed. There was no matter, no solids, no liquids and no gases. There were no tiny specks of dust, no quarks, no electrons, no quantum mechanics—Nothing! That is what void means. There was nothing formed into anything. There was just this very cold and empty black hole, "and darkness was upon the face of the deep."

"And the Spirit of God moved upon the face of the waters."

While the deep (universe) was still void of matter or light, "the Spirit of God moved upon the face of the waters." These "waters" were not oceans. They were the biblical symbols for the potential *worlds* of life.

The Spirit of God is the invisible force and the vital essence that is in all that is alive: mind, consciousness and soul. In the Bible, the Spirit (uppercase) is that which pertains to God, and is God. The spirit (lower case) is that which comes *from* God and that pertains to all life. The word *Spirit* in this verse was written in the singular to emphasize that we are all ONE, and that all life comes from the same source.

Jesus said to his disciples in *The Books of the Saviour* that we are all made of the same "Mixture."[1]

When "the Spirit of God moved upon the face of the waters," Life from the Light called God moved down into the central sphere of what was to become heaven and earth, but was one at the time.

Water, in the Bible, is a symbol for life; the celestial invisibles have *spiritual water*, and all terrestrial life depends on H_2O. The *waters* of heaven and earth are the worlds of the hosts of heaven and humankind of the cosmos. Heaven and Earth have nations and principalities, dominions and powers, and the Spirit of God moved upon what was to come.

> And he said to me, The waters which you saw...are peoples, and multitudes, and nations, and tongues. Revelations 17:15

The spirits and the waters of heaven were the first to be created while the deepest part of God remained dark and empty.

The earliest civilization that we know of, the Sumerians (thousands of years BC), told us from their tablets of stone that *Enlil* had separated the waters of heaven and earth, and that all life was born of the water.

A papyrus was discovered in Egypt that had been written in 311 BC on the story of creation. It told of how *Rã* came into being. The desire to create the heavens and the earth arose in his heart or mind. At the time nothing existed except the vast mass of celestial waters (which the Egyptians call *Nu*), and in this existed the germs of all living things that subsequently took form in heaven and earth.[2]

The early Egyptians believed that this mass of water was in the sky shrouded in darkness, and that *Rã* separated the heavenly waters from those of the earth.

In the Secret Book of John (not in the Bible), John the disciple writes: "The fount of the Spirit flowed out from the living water of light. And it supplied all Aeons and all worlds in every way."[3]

In ancient manuscripts from Jewish sources, Aeons (with an uppercase *A*) was a name given to the many levels of heaven.

> *"And God said, Let there be light: and there was light. And God saw the light, that it was good: and God divided the light from the darkness."*

NOW creation begins! As the rays of light penetrated the blackness of the "deep," there were streaks and flashes of energy and light as "God divided the light from the darkness." Science refers to this moment in time as *The Big Bang* and the Bible appears to corroborate that.

> The LORD also thundered in the heavens, and the Highest gave his voice; hail stones and coals of fire…he sent out his arrows, and scattered them; and he shot out lightnings and discomfited them. Then the channels of waters were seen, and the foundations of the world were discovered… . Psalm 18:13–15

Energy is vast and complex, and the phenomena of light, visible and invisible, is multiform. It is light that permeates and engages the cosmos. Without light there would be no creation for all creation *is* light (energy), and before there was light on the scene the potential earth was without form and void.

As various forces of light and energy streaked through the universe, the natural law of evolution processed the energy into matter and it became the dust of the earth. There were explosions and implosions, and pieces and chunks of burning flint were hurled into space.

Over the eons, matter was formed into stellar bodies that revolved, rotated, and collided. After many more eons, they developed their own patterns and orbits, and became planets and moons or just plain rocks without any light of their own. Some of these would become awash with water and intermittent starlight and darkness, and would be known in biblical terms as *the many waters*.

> Tremble, thou earth, at the presence of the LORD...Which turned the rock into a standing water, the flint into a fountain of waters.
> Psalm 114:7–8

(When light struck into the universe and divided the darkness, rock was the first solid that was formed.)

> Who has measured the waters in the hollow of his hand, and meted out heaven with the span, and comprehended the dust of the earth in a measure...? Isaiah 40:12

> And I heard as it were the voice of a great multitude, and as the voice of many waters.... Revelation 19:6

> The voice of the LORD is upon the waters: the God of glory thunders: the LORD is upon many waters. Psalm 29:3

It is evident that the properties of liquid water have been designed expressly to accommodate life. We live on a watery planet (70.8% water), we live in a body that is mostly water, and all life depends on water for survival. There can be no better symbol of life.

According to the King James Bible, there are many watery planets like ours, more than can be numbered—like the "sand of the sea."

The Scriptures sometimes refer to the empty spaces of the cosmos as *the sea* and the many waters are sometimes described as *the isles of the sea* or as *the fountains of waters*.

> ...and worship him that made heaven, and earth, and the sea, and the fountains of waters.... Revelation 14:7

> ...the isles, and the inhabitants thereof. Isaiah 42:10

Every planet that harbors life has a "tent" that surrounds it—like the oxygen tent that encloses our world. They must indeed look like fountains in the inhospitable regions of the cosmos or like islands of refuge in a vast dark sea.

> It is he that sits upon the circle of the earth, and the inhabitants of it are as grasshoppers; that stretches out the heavens as a curtain, and spreads them out as a tent to dwell in. Isaiah 40:22

> Wisdom: The LORD possessed me in the beginning of his way, before his works of old. I was set up from everlasting, from the beginning, or ever the earth was...While as yet he had not made the earth...nor the highest part of the dust of the world...I was daily his delight...Rejoicing in the habitable part of his earth; and my delights were with the sons of men. Proverbs 8:22–31

> He has made the earth by his power, he has established the world by his wisdom, and has stretched out the heaven by his understanding. When he utters his voice, there is a multitude of waters in the heavens; and he causes the vapours to ascend from the ends of the earth: he makes lightnings with rain, and brings forth the wind out of his treasures. Jeremiah 51:15–16

When God said, "Let there be light," he extended his Light into the cold, black depth, and matter was created. However, the universe is still very black because the light is only "divided" from the darkness, and there was a reason for that.

"And God called the light Day, and the darkness he called Night."

Of the many forms of light, invisible and visible, the light that was made to divide the darkness would give all life in the universe a day and a night—for periods of activity and periods of rest. It would also give us *Time*.

"And the evening and the morning were the first day."

"...evening and morning..." We tend to think of morning and evening as a wakeful day and readers have always wondered why the Bible calls a day "evening and morning" that to us would be a night. Somewhere in ancient Jewish ritual, however, the concept of what constitutes a day was different from ours. The writer of the creation story was, without a doubt, a very religious Jew, and whether it was Moses remains in question, but he was an extraordinary human being. He had the science of creation in perfect order and accuracy, and he combined his truly inspired knowledge into the art of poetry and prose with the symbology and soul of a mystic. The term of *evening and morning* that he used also suggests that he may have been a priest.

The *Shema*, the fundamental prayer of Judaism, was recited in the evening, "...when you lie down, and when you arise... ." (Deuteronomy 6:7)

The Babylonian Talmud begins with "From what time in the evening may the Shema be recited? From the time the priests may begin to eat of their heave-offering [consecrated food], until the end of the first watch."

Over the centuries, there was much controversy and wrangling among the sages of the various Talmudic writings, and there was no clear answer as to how a day should be measured or why evening was emphasized, or even when it was first proposed. I will, therefore, settle for the written word of the *Mishnah*:

From the time the priests may begin to eat of their heave-offerings at the day's end, the priests considered themselves unclean, and had to undergo a necessary immersion process. Only then could they eat, and only after the stars appeared in the sky.

In early Jewish tradition, the night also was part of the day, and was divided into three *watches*. The fourth watch was the morning, and the end of the day.[4]

"...evening and the morning were the first day."

That first day was not a Sunday. It was not the first day of the week. It was not a 24-hour day. It was not even a *day*.

That first day in Genesis, and the six days thereafter, when God created the heaven and the earth, was not measured in our time. It was God's time, and his days are measured in eons: time without numbers.

Jesus tells his initiates of the dissolution of the universe after its expansion is completed "in the years of the light." Mary Magdalene asks him:

> "My Lord, how many years of the years of the world is a year of the light?"
>
> Jesus answered: "A day of the light is a thousand years in the world, so that thirty-six myriads of years and a half myriad of years of the world are a single year of the light."[5]

The word *myriad* means that the number is so great that it is indefinite and innumerable.

> ...be not ignorant of this one thing, that one day is with the Lord as a thousand years, and a thousand years as one day. 2 Peter 3:8

"Be not ignorant"

> For a thousand years in your sight are but as yesterday when it is past, and as a watch in the night. Psalm 90:4

After the Spirit of God had moved over the face of the potential waters and streaks and flashes of light entered the black depth of the universe, the natural law of evolution processed the energy into matter—the dust of the earth. It took time, eons of time, and it was God's time—one day!

> Everything moves in the universe. Nothing stands still...and created things run their courses, and do their works, and they know not how to stand idle.... (Solomon Ode 16)[6]

> Shall the earth be made to bring forth in one day? or shall a nation be born at once? Isaiah 66:8

> All these things you did establish in your wisdom. You did appoint all your works before ever creating them...the host of your spirits and the congregation of your Holy Ones, the heavens and all their hosts and the earth and all it brings forth. In the seas and the deeps...and an everlasting task; for you have established them before eternity...For you have shown them that which they had not seen by removing all ancient things and creating new ones, by breaking

> asunder things anciently established and raising up the things of eternity. For you are from the beginning and shall endure for ages without end. And you have appointed all these things in the mysteries of your wisdom to make known your glory.
>
> (*The Dead Sea Scrolls: The Hymns*)[7]

"…for you have shown them that which they have not seen, by removing all ancient things and creating new ones, by breaking asunder things anciently established… ." Evolution!

All creatures create. We create because God created; it's the God in us. Whether it's a web, a nest or a palace, creativity begins with a *thought*. Without an image in the mind, without a vision, there can be no creation. With creation a tangible something comes into existence, a product that takes time...and energy. It evolves. Nothing that is made of matter in the universe is created instantaneously. Matter forms and grows from other matter. Matter grows old, wears out, or deteriorates, and dies, and new matter comes into existence. That is how God created the earth. It is the natural, earthly law of God the Father and Mother Nature.

> *And God said, Let there be a firmament in the midst of the waters, and let it divide the waters from the waters.*
> *And God made the firmament, and divided the waters which were under the firmament from the waters which were above the firmament: and it was so.*
> *And God called the firmament Heaven. And the evening and the morning were the second day.*
>
> Genesis 1:6–8

The Second Day

During the first day of the eons after the Spirit of Life had moved over the central sphere of God, the waters of the invisibles came into existence. Further into the depth of complete darkness, a light flashed and was followed by a big bang. The light that streaked through the universe, over time, transformed into the elements of matter.

Then during the second day of eons, a barrier of light was formed between the celestial area of Light and the terrestrial sea of darkness and within the sea of darkness the waters of the cosmos began to evolve.

God divided the waters under the firmament from the waters above the firmament because the waters above were of a different form of energy than the waters below. He made the waters above, "his throne" and he called it *Heaven*, and the waters below he called *Earth*.

> He holds back the face of his throne, and spreads his cloud upon it. He has compassed the waters with bounds, until the day and night come to an end. Job 26:9 – 10

(The day and night: the expansion and contraction of the cosmos.)

> When he gave to the sea his decree, that the waters should not pass his commandment: when he appointed the foundations of the earth: Proverbs 8:29

> Thus says God the LORD, he that created the heavens, and stretched them out; he that spread forth the earth, and that which comes out of it; he that gives breath to the people upon it, and spirit to them that walk therein: Isaiah 42:5

> The earth is the LORD's, and the fulness thereof; the world, and they that dwell therein. For he has founded it upon the seas, and established it upon the floods. Psalm 24:1 – 2

> You, even you, are LORD alone; you have made heaven, the heaven of heavens, with all their host, the earth, and all things that are in it, the seas, and all that is in them, and you preserve them all; and the host of heaven worship you. Nehemiah 9:6

After the second day of time when the heaven of heavens was established and divided from the depth by a firmament of light, there is no more said about heaven in the creation story. From that point on, Genesis concentrates on earth in general and our world in particular. After all, it is a book specifically given to our planet.

And God said, Let the waters under the heaven be gathered together unto one place, and let the dry land appear: and it was so.
And God called the dry land Earth; and the gathering together of the waters called he Seas: and God saw that it was good.
And God said, Let the earth bring forth grass, the herb yielding seed, and the fruit tree yielding fruit after his kind, whose seed is in itself, upon the earth: and it was so.
And the earth brought forth grass, and herb yielding seed after his kind, and the tree yielding fruit, whose seed was in itself, after his kind: and God saw that it was good.
And the evening and the morning were the third day.

Genesis 1:9–13

The Third Day

> *"Let the waters under the heaven be gathered together unto one place...."*

The terrestrial waters in the universe, as did all matter, started out in one spot and "he sent his arrows, and scattered them." (Psalm 18:13–15). The heavens were in the early stages of evolving and developing atmospheres around the cooling rocks and they were still "gathered together unto one place."

> By the word of the LORD were the heavens made...He gathers the waters of the sea together as a heap: he lays up the depth in storehouses. Psalm 33:6–7

> (God)...made the cloud the garment thereof, and thick darkness a swaddlingband for it.... Job 38:9

You have formed the earth and the world. Psalm 90:2

"*. . . and let the dry land appear. . . And God called the dry land Earth; and the gathering together of the waters called he Seas. . . .*"

The first time a word that has a double meaning is mentioned in the Bible it is capitalized. Thereafter, it becomes lowercase. For example, the first mention of Day and Night is capitalized, but thereafter they are not, and the same is true for Cherubim, Heaven, Earth, and Sea.

Earth (uppercase *E*)—the habitable areas of the many waters, *and* the cosmic home of humankind.

Sea (uppercase *S*)—the oceans of the planets from which all life originated, *and* the dark, enveloping space around the fountains of waters and the isles of the sea.

Before the rocky planets were ready to spawn life they were covered in water. They were truly watery planets. Then, over the millennia, the water would recede and the dry land appeared. That is the way our world started out according to science, and that, according to the Bible, is the way of all the worlds.

To him that stretched out the earth above the waters. . . .
Psalm 136:6

The sea is his, and he made it: and his hands formed the dry land.
Psalm 95:5

Who laid the foundations of the earth. . . You covered it with the deep as with a garment; the waters stood above the mountains. At your rebuke they fled; at the voice of your thunder they hastened away. They go up by the mountains; they go down by the valleys unto a place which you have founded for them. You have set a boundary that they may not pass over; that they turn not again to cover the earth. Psalm 104:5–9

The cosmos was expanding. The waterlogged rocks, along with the immature bodies of fire, gases and lightning, were small, oddly shaped, and close together. Those fragments and flints, that would have been the earliest bodies of matter to form, eventually turned into stars, planets and galaxies, and they are what our astronomers would now give anything to observe, as they probe the universe with ever increasingly powerful telescopes.

Those planets would have been the first of the many waters to evolve: the first and the oldest civilizations, and by far the most advanced. They would be eons ahead of us, and most of them would still be out there somewhere, deep in the middle of the expanding cosmos.

Some, however, may no longer exist. As the cosmos evolves, stellar bodies die, and new ones are born, and that is the natural law of all that is called *matter*, or *earth*. Everything evolves and changes over time. "Nothing stands idle," as Solomon said.

Just recently, astronomers watched with fascination as the Hubble Telescope sent an image of a distant galaxy smashing into, and being *eaten* by, a much larger galaxy and the fiery carnage disappearing into a black hole. I couldn't help but wonder about the life within those galaxies. What would it be like if the Milky Way collided with another galaxy? Would we be aware of what was happening?

We have so many questions. We are so young geologically and astronomically in the grand scheme of things, and so small and seemingly insignificant.

> Behold, the nations are as a drop of a bucket, and are counted as the small dust of the balance: behold, he takes up the isles as a very little thing. Isaiah 40:15

> "...*Let the earth bring forth grass, the herb...and the fruit tree...And the earth brought forth...after his kind*... ."

> The winds come forth from your nostrils, and the celestial water from your mouth...You make the earth to bring forth fruit so that gods and men may have abundance...You are the great god that stretched out the heavens, You make the Disk to revolve...you are the fashioner of gods and men, and of everything which exists...you make the grain to come forth... .[8]

> He causes the grass to grow for the cattle, and herb for the service of man: that he may bring forth food out of the earth; and wine that makes glad the heart of man, and oil to make his face shine, and bread which strengthens man's heart. The trees of the LORD are full of sap; the cedars of Lebanon...where the birds make their nests.... Psalm 104:14–17

> God gives it a body as it has pleased him, and to every seed his own body. 1 Corinthians 15:38

God did *not* say, "let there be grass." God said, "Let the earth bring forth grass... ." And it was the earth that brought forth, through the process of light-energy into chemical energy, that laid the groundwork for the formation of the cell.

ooo

The waters that contained the spirit of life, and that had covered the planet as a garment, was now into oceans, rivers and lakes. The germs of life from the waters had saturated the dry ground, and the earth would, eventually, bring forth first the grasses and the herbs and then the trees, after their kind.

All plants reproduce after their kind, but the planet is round and has many climactic regions. Plants of all kinds have *learned* to adapt. It is called *evolution*. "And to every seed his own body" that will serve it best.

> *And God said, Let there be lights in the firmament of the heaven to divide the day from the night; and let them be for signs, and for seasons, and for days, and years.*
> *And let them be for lights in the firmament of the heaven to give light upon the earth: and it was so.*
> *And God made two great lights; the greater light to rule the day, and the lesser light to rule the night: he made the stars also.*
> *And God set them in the firmament of the heaven to give light upon the earth.*
>
> Genesis 1:14–17

> *And to rule over the day and over the night, and to divide the light from the darkness: and God saw that it was good. And the evening and the morning were the fourth day.*
>
> Genesis 1:18–19

The Fourth Day

The fiery rocks that had flashed with lightning and gases and spun uncontrollably became stabilized into their own revolutions and orbits. Their predictable patterns, and those of rocks which had no light of their own, established a cosmos that would give humankind of the many waters a life-sustaining earth to live on.

It is the stars, and especially that all-important star—the sun—that not only give us signs and seasons and days and years, but also give us our material bodies, all that is on our fragment of earth, and earth itself. We are stardust.

> He appointed the moon for seasons: the sun knows his going down. You make darkness, and it is night: wherein all the beasts of the forest do creep forth. The young lions roar after their prey, and seek their meat from God. The sun rises, they gather themselves together, and lay them down in their dens. Man goes forth to his work and to his labour until evening. O LORD, how manifold are your works! In wisdom have you made them all: the earth is full of your riches.
>
> Psalm 104:19–24

> When I consider your heavens, the work of your fingers, the moon and the stars, which you have ordained.... Psalm 8:3

> Can you bind the sweet influences of Pleiades, or loose the bands of Orion? Can you bring forth Mazzaroth in his season? or can you guide Arcturus [the bear] with his sons [his train]? Do you know the ordinances of heaven? Can you set their dominion in the earth?
>
> Job 38:31–33

> There is one glory of the sun, and another glory of the moon, and another glory of the stars: for one star differs from another star in glory. 1 Corinthians 15:41

The dry faces of the cosmic earth that had already begun to "bring forth" the germination of grasses, herbs and trees (that would eventually cover the rocky worlds with a lush carpet of green) would not have needed a well-positioned sun to get them started. Plants like algae and lichen can grow in extreme climactic conditions. All the germs of life needed were the elements and chemicals of water.

> *"And let them be for lights in the firmament of heaven... ."*

This was heaven with no s, but the reference is not being made to the heaven of the invisibles. The cosmos is the *heavens*, but at that moment in time it had just begun to expand and all that was the cosmos was in one small area of the universe. There was only one earthly heaven. Then, as time passed (eons of time), more matter was formed into stars, planets, moons and galaxies, and the cosmos expanded and became *the heavens*. They took their appointed places in the black depth of the universe "for signs, and for seasons, and for days, and years." And they truly are all of these for each of the worlds and their individual *first heaven*.

> You have increased the nation, O LORD...you have removed it far unto all the ends of the earth. Isaiah 26:15

> You did cleave the fountain and the flood: you dried up the mighty rivers. The day is yours, the night also is yours: you have prepared the light and the sun. You have set all the borders of the earth: you have made summer and winter. Psalm 74:15–17

The following two verses seem to suggest that at some stage of development the planets may have gone through their world covering ice ages.

> He sends forth his commandment upon earth: his word runs very swiftly. He gives snow like wool; he scatters the hoarfrost like ashes.

> He casts forth his ice like morsels: who can stand before his cold? He sends out his word, and melts them: he causes his wind to blow, and the waters to flow. Psalm 147:15–18

> Out of whose womb came the ice? And the hoary frost of heaven, who has gendered it? The waters are hid as with a stone, and the face of the deep is frozen. Job 38:29–30

The stars were evolving and some had become life-nourishing suns to the family of planets. The cosmos was now rapidly expanding, as flaming bodies of matter were being flung out into the darkness. The many waters and their suns, moons and companion dry planets became engulfed within the seas of galaxies and were driven farther and farther away from each other.

> Woe to the multitude of many people, which make a noise like the noise of the seas: and to the rushing of nations, that make a rushing like the rushing of mighty waters! The nations shall rush like the rushing of many waters: but God shall rebuke them, and they shall flee far off, and shall be chased as the chaff of the mountains before the wind, and like a rolling thing before the whirlwind.
>
> Isaiah 17:12–13

Over time and space that cannot be numbered or measured, our planet became one of the specks of dust of the black and cold depth. Our planet and the other many waters are "as the sand of the seashore" in the great scheme of creation.

> Lest you lift up your eyes unto heaven, and when you see the sun, and the moon, and the stars, even all the host of heaven, should be driven to worship them, and serve them, which the LORD your God has divided unto all the nations under the whole heaven.
>
> Deuteronomy 4:19

> ...Let the earth hear, and all that is therein...the world, and all things that come forth of it.... Isaiah 34:1

> Through faith we understand that the worlds were framed by the word of God.... Hebrews 11:3

> O God...who is the confidence of all the ends of the earth, and of them that are afar off upon the sea...which stills the noise of their waves, and the tumult of the people.... Psalm 65:5–7

Although all humans throughout the universe live on mere specks of dust and we are but dust ourselves, humankind is the most precious in God's eyes. It was for us that he created the heaven and the earth, and he created us for his pleasure. (Psalm 149:4; Proverbs 8:22–31). After each stage of development and after each *days* end, God looked it over and "saw that it was good."

> If I take the wings of the morning, and dwell in the uttermost parts of the sea; even there shall your hand lead me.... Psalm 139:9

> God, who at sundry times and in divers manners [numerous times and various ways] spoke in times past to the fathers by the prophets, has in these last days spoken to us by his Son, whom he has appointed heir of all things, by whom also he made the worlds.
>
> Hebrews 1:2

And God said, Let the waters bring forth abundantly the moving creature that has life, and fowl that may fly above the earth in the open firmament of heaven.
And God created great whales, and every living creature that moves, which the waters brought forth abundantly, after their kind, and every winged fowl after his kind: and God saw that it was good.
And God blessed them, saying, Be fruitful, and multiply, and fill the waters in the seas, and let fowl multiply in the earth.
And the evening and the morning were the fifth day.

Genesis 1:20–23

The Fifth Day

"Let the waters bring forth. . . ." means that *all* of the waters in the cosmos brought forth the moving creature. And it also means that from the water comes "the moving creature that has life." All earthly life came from the water, just as the unborn slumbers in its embryonic microcosm of water.

Earlier in this chapter, we read that the ancient Egyptian's creation story told that all life originated from the vast mass of celestial waters in the sky called *Nu*, and in this existed the germs of all living things that subsequently took form in heaven and earth.

Evolution was similar throughout the many waters. Some of those planets may be ahead of us by millions of years, and there may be worlds that are less advanced than we are, but time and distance are nothing in the grand scheme of creation. All of the many waters would still be within the range of the six days of "Let there be. . .and there was. . .and God saw that it was good."

> The LORD looks from heaven; and beholds all the sons of men. From the place of his habitation he looks upon all the inhabitants of the earth. He fashioned their hearts alike; he considers all their works. Psalm 33:13–15

> God. . .has made of one blood all nations of men to dwell on all the face of the earth, and has determined the times before appointed, and the bounds of their habitation. Acts 17:26

Genesis tells us that all of the life-sustaining planets evolved the same way. We can, however, from here on in, concentrate on our own world and its development over the millennia.

When the first creatures were born of the water on our planet there was only one ocean and one mass of land named *Pangaea*. Scientists have theorized that life began in the water more than 600 million years ago during the Precambrian period. In the Bible it was known as the *fifth day*.

The water on our globe had receded into an ocean, lakes and rivers. There are days and nights and seasons. It was only after the plant life had established itself, both in the water and on the soggy and gaseous land, that there would be food for the moving creature in the water and the fowl of the air.

Whether the first moving creature, as distinct from the non-moving plant, evolved from the same chemical recipe, the Bible does not say, but there really is not that much difference between us and our houseplants. We all have to breathe and we all have to drink. We all have bodies made up of cells, and the earliest stages of the embryo of a rat, a human, and a bean are similar in appearance.

In the oceans of our planet, there are animals that resemble and have some characteristics of plants and there are plants that resemble animals. Then we have the sponge that is a plant and an animal, as is the bacterium. The virus is alive, but is neither plant nor animal.

When the Spirit of God moved over the waters, there was no separate spirit for plants, animals or humans; it was spirit in the singular. All life is ONE.

A Jewish legend of the fourth century AD called the *Haggadah*, from an early Kabbalah writing, tells of a most remarkable creature known as *man of the mountain.*

> His form was exactly that of a human being, but he is fastened to the ground by means of a navel-string, upon which his life depends. Once the cord is snapped, he dies. This "animal" kept himself alive from what was produced by the soil around him. No creature may venture to approach…for he seizes and demolishes whatever comes in his reach. To kill him…the navel-string must be severed from a distance by means of a dart, and then he dies amid groans and moans.[9]

It is only a legend, but like all legends and myths that have come down to us over the centuries, there are sometimes elements of truth. Yes, they are woven with colorful threads and embroidered with vivid imaginations, but we still have creations in our oceans today that could make for a good myth or legend. We do have plants on land rooted to the ground that entice insects with their scent or flavor and then hold them tight while they ingest them.

There could have been plants like that in ancient times, and may still have been around after humankind appeared on the scene. They might have been bigger than today's species and able to trap small animals; and to the people of the time they may have seemed like they were part animal.

The writings tell of other such creatures in different forms and situations, and the people were in a moral dilemma as to what they should do. If they killed one of these *creatures*, should it be a sacrificial killing as they would an animal, or should they just chop it down as one would a plant?

O O O

Now in day five of the eons and before there were mammals and humans, the world of water and land was covered in greenery. There may have been trees that are much larger than those we have today and other kinds of giant plants as well, both on land and in the water. The planet was lush, no doubt about it; our coal and oil reserves are evidence of that.

Just as there was giant plant life in the water and on land when our planet was very young, from the waters of our oceans there came to be huge creatures. The Bible refers to one of these monsters as *leviathan*. This was not a whale, as some scholars have proposed. The whale was mentioned on occasion as a creature separate from the leviathan, and if it had been the same animal, the translators would have given it one name—not two. The description of them is also quite different. The whale, in the Bible, was a big fish, whereas the leviathan was a huge dragon, serpent or reptile and was always fierce and dangerous.

> The LORD speaks to Job: Can you draw out leviathan with a hook?...None is so fierce that dare stir him up...I will not conceal his parts, nor his power, nor his comely proportion...his teeth are terrible round about...His scales are his pride, shut up together as with a close seal. One is so near to another, that no air can come between them...His sneezings flash forth light, and his eyes are like the eyelids of the morning [fast blinking]...Out of his mouth go burning lamps and sparks of fire leap out...Out of his nostrils goes smoke...When he raises himself up, the mighty are afraid...The arrow cannot make him flee: slingstones are turned with him into rubble...He makes the deep to boil like a pot...Upon earth there is none like him, who is made without fear.
>
> Job 41:1–33

> By his spirit he has garnished the heavens; his hand has formed the crooked serpent.... Job 26:13

> O LORD, how manifold are your works...So is this great and wide sea, wherein are things creeping inumerable, both small and great beasts...there is the leviathan, whom you have made to play therein...You give them their meat in due season...You hide their face...you take away their breath, they die, and return to their dust...You send forth your spirit, they are created and you renew the face of the earth. Psalm 104:24–30

"You hide their face..." means that the form they had is no more. "you renew the face of the earth," means that new forms come into existence as old forms and faces die and return to dust. Here we see a perfect description of evolution.

The early Egyptians, as did most other nations, had many legends of land and sea monsters in the form of reptiles, snakes and scorpions and almost always associated them with evil forces. Besides the creatures of the sea, they also had legends of *winged serpents* with the most terrifying features. Today we have dug out from the cliffs, the hills and the ancient river valleys, some of these fossils. We call them *dinosaurs.*

Phil Currie, a paleontologist at the Tyrrell Museum of Paleontology in Alberta, Canada, said, "It's not that birds descended from dinosaurs; it's that birds *are* dinosaurs."

The King James Bible said it first. "And the waters brought forth...every winged fowl after his kind...."

> On the same day with the fishes, the birds were created, for these two kinds of animals are closely related to each other.[10]

> *And God said, Let the earth bring forth the living creature after his kind, cattle, and creeping thing, and beast of the earth after his kind: and it was so.*
> *And God made the beast of the earth after his kind, and cattle after their kind, and everything that creeps upon the earth after his kind: and God saw that it was good.*
> Genesis 1:24–25

And God said, Let us make man in our image, after our likeness: and let them have dominion over the fish of the sea, and over the fowl of the air, and over the cattle, and over all the earth, and over every creeping thing that creeps upon the earth.
So God created man in his own image, in the image of God created he him; male and female created he them.
And God blessed them, and God said unto them, Be fruitful, and multiply, and replenish the earth, and subdue it: and have dominion over the fish of the sea, and over the fowl of the air, and over every living thing that moves upon the earth.
And God said, Behold, I have given you every herb bearing seed, which is upon the face of all the earth, and every tree, in which is the fruit of a tree yielding seed; to you it shall be for meat.
And to every beast of the earth, and to every fowl of the air, and to everything that creeps upon the earth, wherein there is life, I have given every green herb for meat: and it was so.
And God saw everything that he had made, and, behold, it was very good. And the evening and the morning were the sixth day.

Genesis 1:26–31

The Sixth Day

The Journals *Nature* and *Science* recently reported that a team of scientists had discovered, in a bed of rock in a mine in Southern China, what they believed to be the fossils of complex animal life. Along with an abundance of the earliest marine seaweed and sponges, were very well preserved animal embryos the size of a grain of sand, but already at the level of individual cells.

The embryos belonged to a group called *bilaterians*, and are more complex than that of some of the marine life such as jellyfish and sponges. Bilaterian is the lineage from which we eventually originated. It is not known what kind of animals these fossils would have become. The Precambrian algae that were found alongside the embryos had already attained much of their anatomical and reproductive features that are seen in modern ocean plants.

The age of this discovery has been estimated at approximately 570 million years (the dawn of the *sixth day*). Over the eons the creatures evolved and multiplied, "and God saw that it was good."

About 200 million years ago, when the land of Pangaea began to break up, continents were formed and the ocean became divided by masses of land. Both the life that moved and the life that was rooted in the soil spread out over the globe. By now there must have been quite a variety of species, but the most noticeable and fearsome would have been the giants of water, land and air.

As I have mentioned, ancient people from almost all nations and races had many stories to tell about how, when the world was young and ruled by the gods, there were dragons, four-footed serpents and giant birds and animals. Down through the generations, the stories became more vivid and the creatures more grotesque, and most of them were thought to be evil personified, such as Satan—the serpent.

The snake of today is a subtle animal that strikes with the speed of lightning. Those serpents and dragons of ancient times were large and uncontrollable, and the legends tell us that they had to be destroyed by the Creator or they would have destroyed the world. Had they been allowed to live, they would eventually have eaten all the food and drunk the rivers dry. Today we know that the dinosaur fossils we find were the serpents and dragons of legends and mythology. How would the people of the past have known about them? Did they perhaps find the odd fossil? Did their gods tell them?

In both *The King James Bible* and *The Revised English Bible*, the leviathan is noted as a crocodile and the behemoth as a hippopotamus. These animals are still with us, but the leviathan and the behemoth are not. The Bible and Haggadah (a Jewish legend) explain what happened to them:

> Behold now behemoth, which I made with you; [on the sixth day] he eats grass as an ox. Lo now, his strength is in his loins, and the force is in the navel of his belly. He moves his tail like a cedar: the sinew of his stones are wrapped together. His bones are as strong pieces of brass; his bones are like bars of iron. He is the chief of the ways of God: he that made him can make his sword to approach

> him. Surely the mountains bring him forth food, where all the beasts of the field play. He lies under the shady trees...The shady trees cover him with their shadow; the willows of the brook cover him...He drinks up a river, he hurries not: He trusts that he can draw up Jordan in his mouth.... . Job 40:15–24

God made this creature and only the force of God (his sword) can destroy him.

In Ezekiel 29:4–5, Pharaoh is referred to as a dragon of the sea, and the LORD will deal with him as he once did with the dragon:

> But I will put hooks in your jaws and I will cause the fish of your rivers to stick to your scales...and I will bring you up out of the midst of your rivers...and I will leave you thrown into the wilderness...you shall fall upon the open fields, you shall not be brought together, nor gathered. I have given you for meat to the beasts of the fields and to the fowls of heaven.

> You broke the head of the dragons in the waters...You broke the heads of leviathan in pieces, and gave them to be meat to the people of the wilderness. Psalm 74:13–14

"The dragons in the waters" is the evil forces that are in the worlds of the cosmos (the waters). The heads of evil will be broken, just as the leviathan was destroyed and became meat for those in the wilderness (the wild species of animals that would in time become man).

> In that day, the LORD with his sore and great and strong sword shall punish leviathan the piercing serpent, even leviathan that crooked serpent; and he shall slay the dragon that is in the sea.
> Isaiah 27:1

In this verse too, the serpents and dragon are personified as evil spirits that have overtaken the world like these animals once did in ages past.

The Jewish legend Haggadah tells us more:

> Nor is this world inhabited by man the first of things earthly created by God. He made several worlds before ours, but he destroyed them all, because he was pleased with none until he created ours...if God in his goodness had not given protection to the weak, the tame animals would have been extirpated long ago by the wild animals [and] the strength of behemoth...he roars so loud that all the animals hear it...and for a whole year they are affrighted and timid...the great bird Ziz flaps his wings and utters his cry, so that the...eagles and the vultures, blench, and they fear to swoop down upon the others...And again, were it not for the goodness of God, the vast number of big fish had quickly put an end to the little ones. But at the time of the winter solstice...the sea grows restless, for then leviathan spouts up water, and the big fish become uneasy. They restrain their appetite, and the little ones escape their rapacity.[11]

> The ruler over the sea animals is leviathan. With all the other fishes he was made on the fifth day. Originally he was created male and female like all the others animals. But when it appeared that a pair of these monsters might annihilate the whole earth with their united strength, God killed the female. So enormous is leviathan that to quench his thirst he needs all the water that flows from the Jordan into the sea. His food consists of the fish which go between his jaws of their own accord. When he is hungry, a hot breath blows from his nostrils, and it makes the waters of the great sea seething hot. Formidable though behemoth, the other monster, is, he feels insecure until he is certain leviathan has satisfied his thirst... .[12]

During the dinosaur age there existed a sea lizard known to scientists as a *mosasaur*. It was ten metres in length with a metre-long jaw. In 1997 two researchers, one from the University of Alberta and the other from the University of Sydney, spent a year studying a 97 million-year-old fossil that was a metre long with small hind legs. The two men believe that this creature and the mosasaur are related and may be the ancestors of the modern snake.

In the story of the garden of Eden (I will discuss this in Chapter Six), the snake supposedly had legs until it was cursed to crawl on its belly for the rest of its days on earth.

King Nebuchadnezzar (605–562 BC):

> I established Babylon, the sublime city...On the threshold of her gates, I set huge bulls and footed serpents, such as no other king before had wrought... .[13]

On the evening of the sixth day of the eons the dinosaurs were no more. It is believed that the big guys died out some 65 million years ago, and their demise is still a contentious issue amongst scientists. How did they die? And why? Maybe Jewish legend has the only plausible explanation for their extinction —some of them were just too big, and they could drink the rivers dry.

Now the animal kingdom was complete, as the earth brought forth the mammals and creeping things after their kind. Whether the creeping things were insects or small rodents, the Bible doesn't say. I would tend to think it would be the latter and that insects would have evolved with the oceanic life on the fifth day.

Down through the ages of the sixth day, the creatures of land, sea and air evolved, and God continually renewed the earth as some species died out. The material tree of life on this planet branched out into innumerable twigs and each bore fruit after its kind.

There were different species of grazing cattle and there were all kinds of beasts of the fields and forests, the hills and mountains. There were the little ones who scampered around and sought safety by digging their homes into the ground, and others that built their homes high up in the trees. And then there was the frisky little fellow who climbed to the top of the giant trees and swung from branch to branch. This was *man.*

Man was one of a *branch* of primates from which a variety of *twigs* of different shapes and sizes, and levels of intelligence, had evolved.

Man had evolved to the stage where it could climb, grasp onto things with its front limbs, and toss rocks and fruit at other passing creatures. On occasion, this hairy little creature tried to stand on its hind legs and walk.

When some of these primates got too big to climb trees, their tails were lost through the process of evolution. Some of these tailless species became a little smarter while down on the ground and they began to chisel stones into spears, chase other animals, and eat them.

"And God said, Let us make man in our image, after our likeness...So God created man in his own image, in the image of God created he him: male and female created he them.... ."

To understand this verse, let us first answer the piercing question: Who was God *talking* to? "Let *us* make man in *our* image... ."

This verse has been a thorn in the flesh for the Bible reader and scholar alike because it has always been supposed that God was all alone up there, sitting on his golden throne. (Remember, God has no shape or form and cannot be seen, nor has anyone heard his voice.) "In the beginning God created the heaven;" the third heaven, the heaven of heavens, God's throne—where the Lords and the hosts of heaven reside.

God presented his *Thought* to the Lord of Lords; the Son of God; the first begotten Son of all creation and to all the Lords of heaven. It is they who are clothed in light who are the image and likeness of God in soul, mind and consciousness, and who speak for God. It was to them that God said, "Let *us* make man in our *image*... ." that he may have God's likeness in mind, consciousness and soul.

Of the whole world menagerie of creatures that scampered, trotted, flew and swam, God chose a small, cute (or maybe not so cute), curious animal for special development, and its name was *man*.

> When I consider your heavens, the work of your fingers, the moon and the stars, which you have ordained; What is man, that you are mindful of him? and the son of man, that you visit him? For you have made him a little lower than the angels, and have crowned him with glory and honor. You made him to have dominion over the works of your hands; you have put all things under his feet....
>
> Psalm 8:3–6

> Who can endure Your glory, and what is the son of man in the midst of Your wonderful deeds? What shall one born of woman be accounted before You? Kneaded from the dust, his abode is the nourishment of worms. He is but a shape, but molded clay, and inclines toward dust. What shall molded clay reply? What counsel shall it understand. (*The Dead Sea Scrolls: The Community Rule*)[14]

> I, a creature of clay kneaded with water; a heap of dust and a heart of stone. . . . (*The Dead Sea Scrolls: The Hymns*)[15]

Today we find the fossils of early man in various stages of development, of which most became extinct. Others, however, evolved into hominids of several different species. It appears that some of these hominids coexisted in parts of the world, and one theory is that Neanderthal man may have lived in the same area as modern man and may even have interbred. When the primate called *man* became modern (Homo sapiens) is not known, but speculation is that on this planet, as hominids, we may be at least one million years old.

In the magazine *Discover*, there was an article about organ transplants of the future coming from animals. One problem, however, is that when an animal organ is put into a human body, the body rejects it so violently that the organ turns black before the surgeon can even stitch up the patient. The defense mechanism in the body works very quickly against something that is particularly foreign, such as the organ of a pig, sheep or dog. Organs from chimpanzees and baboons, however, are not rejected.

It has been discovered that the brain of a chimpanzee has the same wiring for speech as the human brain, but it has never been developed. They are our closest cousins in the animal kingdom; and they share 98% of their genes with us. No other animal has acquired the brain capacity for human speech. Communication involving speech is one of the attributes that we share with the Creator and the invisibles of heaven.

It stands to reason why one small twig from the primate branch was chosen to "have dominion over the fish of the sea, and over the fowl of the air, and over the cattle, and over all the earth, and over every creeping thing that creeps upon the earth. . . ."

> It is You who have created breath for the tongue and You know its words; You did establish the fruit of the lips before ever they were. You set words to measure and the flow of breath from the lips to metre. You bring forth sounds according to their mysteries, and the flow of breath from the lips according to its reckoning, that they may tell of Your glory and recount Your wonders...and that Your name be praised by the mouth of all men, and that they may know You according to their understanding and bless You forever.
>
> (*The Dead Sea Scrolls: The Hymns*)[16]

> I will praise you; for I am fearfully and wonderfully made...My substance was not hid from you, when I was made in secret, and curiously wrought in the lowest parts of the earth. Your eyes did see my substance, yet being imperfect; and in your book all my members were written, which in continuance were fashioned, when as yet there was none of them. Psalm 139:14–16

> *"And God said...I have given you every herb bearing seed...and every tree, in which is the fruit...to you it shall be for meat. And to every beast of the earth...I have given every green herb for meat... ."*

We were not meant to eat each other. What happened?

> Once upon a time, there was no snake, there was no scorpion...
> There was no fear, no terror. Man had no rival... .
> (An Ancient Sumerian Poem)

NOTES

[1] Mead, G.R.S. (1974). *Pistis Sophia.* Secaucas, NJ: University Books Inc., p. 206.

[2] Budge, E.A.W. (1960). *The Book of the Dead.* New York, NY: University Books., p. 162.

[3] Barnstone, W. (1984). *The Other Bible* San Francisco, CA: Harper Collins Publishers., p. 54.

[4] Goldin, J. (1957). *The Living Talmud.* New York, NY: New American Library., p. 13.

[5] Mead, G.R.S. (1974). *Pistis Sophia.* Secaucas, NJ: University Books Inc., p. 203.

[6] Barnstone, W. (1984). *The Other Bible.* San Francisco, CA: Harper Collins Publishers., p. 277. (This is an old translation no longer in print.)

[7] Vermes, G. (1962). *The Dead Sea Scrolls in English.* London,UK: Penguin Books., p. 191.

[8] Budge, E.A.W. (1960). *The Book of the Dead.* New York, NY: University Books, p. 172.

[9] Barnstone, W. (1984). *The Other Bible.* San Francisco,CA: Harper Collins Publishers., p. 24.

[10] Barnstone, W. (1984). *The Other Bible.* San Francisco,CA: Harper Collins Publishers., p. 23.

[11] Barnstone, W. (1984). *The Other Bible.* San Francisco,CA: Harper Collins Publishers., p. 15.

[12] Barnstone, W. (1984). *The Other Bible.* San Francisco,CA: Harper Collins Publishers., p. 22.

[13] Cottrell, L. (1962). *The Horizon Book of Lost Worlds.* New York, NY: American Heritage Publishing Co., p. 206.

[14] Vermes, G. (1962). *The Dead Sea Scrolls in English.* Middlesex,UK: Penguin Books., p. 94.

[15] Vermes, G. (1962). *The Dead Sea Scrolls in English.* Middlesex,UK: Penguin Books., p.200–201.

[16] Vermes, G. (1962). *The Dead Sea Scrolls in English.* Middlesex,UK: Penguin Books., p.152–153.

3
The Sabbath

> *Thus the heavens and the earth were finished, and all the host of them.*
> *And on the seventh day God ended his work which he had made; and he rested on the seventh day from all his work which he had made.*
> *And God blessed the seventh day, and sanctified it: because that in it he had rested from all his work which God created and made.*
>
> Genesis 2:1–3

WITHIN six days of eons (time without number), God *created* from his Light the elements of heaven and earth. Then he *made* from these elements the *heavens* and the earth through the process of evolution. After the heavens and the earth were finished, he rested from all his work that he *created and made*.

God rested on the seventh day?

God is the Energy of energies. He does not need rest. What this *rest* means is that it is a short pause in the breath of God. The work in the universe was finished, and the cosmos was expanding according to his law of evolution and the element of Time.

God is at rest, and it is still the seventh day.

Nothing has been created since the eve of the sixth day when that funny little primate was given dominion over the earth. Everything was ordained and established, and the earth's foundations were laid, and it has all been evolving ever since. God said: "Let it be...and it was...and let it bring forth...and it brought forth...and it was very good."

The seventh day was intended to be a *day of rest* for all of life and for all time. When the work on this planet was completed it was designed to be a paradise on earth, just like the one in the heaven of heavens. All creatures, great and small, were to live in peace and comfort.

> *"And to every beast of the earth, and to every fowl of the air, and to everything that creeps upon the earth, wherein there is life, I have given every green herb for meat: and it was so."*

All of us were to eat our fruit and vegetables and salads. That's why all that green stuff was created by God the Father, and came forth from Mother Nature.

Somewhere back in time, and hidden in the recesses of ancient memories, this was known, as the Sumerian poem suggests. The poet laments that at one time there was no fear or terror, and, as yet, no snakes or scorpions had evolved.

Life was meant to be quite different than what it has turned out to be, but we dig up the fossils of our caveman ancestors, their tools and spears, and we find that they killed other creatures, and even each other, for food. Spears are not needed to kill vegetables.

Much earlier than that, the dinosaurs and other animals had canine teeth, which indicates that some of them were carnivorous.

The question remains—what happened?

For the answer, we must go back to the meaning of the word *evolution*.

Evolution is a process of unfolding, growing and developing, usually in slow stages—like an embryo in the womb. Within this process, however, a mutation, or sport, can occur. A mutation, or sport, is what happens in a plant or animal that exhibits a sudden and spontaneous variation from the normal specimen on one of its parts.

All of the cosmos and its many waters were created and made to evolve. It is the law of God for the universe. The life forms in the worlds of the cosmos evolved according to their particular situations and climactic conditions, just as our planet has. All of the many waters were made to have a paradise on earth and enjoy the *rest* of God. Perhaps, out there in the vast distance, some accomplished it early in their evolution. Others may have attained this rest only after a long, slow process of evolution, and there might be some planets that, like ours, are still working on it, for what seems like an unattainable goal.

The inhabitants of our watery blue globe developed, quite early, the flesh-eating mutation to crave the junk food of another creature's body. It was carried down through the eons to early man and into this so-called modern era.

Or maybe in this case the term *sport* would be more appropriate. Today we also have, in some humans, the mutation, or *sport*, to kill for pleasure.

We are evolving, but we still have a long way to go.

"God blessed the seventh day, and sanctified it"

Ages passed, and one day Moses climbed to the summit of Mount Sinai with the elders of his people and brought down the commandments for a New World Order. Among the ten most pronounced and basic commandments was: "Remember the sabbath day to keep it holy."

The commandments were first given to the Israelites, as they were the direct lineage from Adam, his son Seth, and down to Noah's son Shem.

From this family tree the Son of God would eventually be born and would present to this wayward planet the original *rest* that was intended for the human race in the beginning.

> Wherefore the children of Israel shall keep the sabbath…throughout their generations, for a perpetual covenant. Exodus 31:16

The meaning of the word *covenant*: An action to recover damages for a breach of contract.

Somewhere in the evolution of this planet there was a mutation, but when mankind became *human* through Adam and Eve with their higher intelligence, mankind was to grow and flourish in the *rest* that God intended. That was what the garden of Eden was all about, and it was taught to our first parents.

Yes, there really was an Adam and an Eve, and there was a garden of Eden.

Over time, however, as the people spread out and multiplied, memories faded and God the Creator was forgotten, along with the blessing of rest.

From vague memories of the subconscious some of the nations of the world would develop and embellish their lives with gods and legends of the spirit world that were somewhere up there in the sky. Some, however, retained much of the original knowledge and may have had peaceful and productive *paradises* on earth for a period of time, and that may be from where the Sumerian poet got his thoughts.

One ethnic group of people who had retained much of the knowledge handed down from Adam—and I say much, but not all—were the Semitic nations, and it was to these people that the commandments and the covenants were first given.

The seventh day was blessed and sanctified in the beginning, but the action was broken and forgotten and now a covenant had to be set up to "remember" the Sabbath.

> Remember the sabbath day to keep it holy. Six days shall you labour, and do all your work: But the seventh day is the sabbath of the LORD your God...For in six days the LORD made heaven and earth, the sea, and all that in them is, and rested the seventh day: wherefore the LORD blessed the sabbath day, and hallowed it... .
>
> Exodus 20:8 – 11

> And the LORD spoke to Moses...When you come into the land which I give you, then shall the land keep a sabbath...Six years shall you sow your field...and gather in the fruit...But the seventh year shall be a sabbath of rest to the land...That which grows of its own accord...you shall not reap...for it is a year of rest... .
>
> Leviticus 25:1 – 5

> ...you shall not do any work, you, nor your son, nor your daughter, your manservant, nor your maidservant, nor your cattle, nor the stranger that is within your gates. Exodus 20:10

There was a good physical reason for the one day of rest every six days. When humankind lost paradise, it had to "work at the sweat of the brow" in order to live on the earth. Without rules and regulations, such as commandments and covenants, all work and no play would be the outcome.

It would have been a way of life then, when people were subject to taskmasters. Still today, even in our civilized countries, we would have employers with whips and seven-day workweeks, although they may no longer have a brow ridge or hairy knuckles.

The LORD God of Israel knew the hearts of the sons of men, and a physical law had to be in place to protect the physical realm: one day of rest out of seven for everyone, every creature, and even the land every seventh year.

Today, we have our days off and our holidays for our physical health and well being, and the various religions have their Sabbath days.

The Sabbath that is observed in the churches, temples and synagogues, however, is bereft of the Holy Spirit. It is only a covenant—an action to recover damages for a breach of contract. It is only a motion—a ritual performed within a religion to bring to the fore a faint memory of what was lost sometime in the beginning.

We do not have the *rest*. What we have is *religion*.

A religion is a formula of laws, practices and rituals set down by one person, or an appointed group of people, for others of like mind to follow. There is nothing wrong with religion if it benefits and serves its people, and the world, but it is not the *rest* that was ordained for all of creation in the beginning of time.

The *rest* that God intended for our planet is, and always has been, available to us and within reach because it is *within us*. Throughout *The King James Bible* it is called *the kingdom of heaven* or *the kingdom of God*.

The *rest* is not a religion—it is a lifestyle.

This is still the seventh day!

> We are spirits from the Spirit:...It is sown a natural body; it is raised a spiritual body. There is a natural body, and there is a spiritual body. 1 Corinthians 15:44

> Come, you blessed of my Father, inherit the kingdom prepared for you from the foundation of the world. Matthew 25:34

> Return to your rest, O my soul...I will walk before the LORD in the land of the living. Psalm 116:7–9

The LORD is the portion of mine inheritance...The lines are fallen to me in pleasant places...I have a good heritage. I have set the LORD always before me: because he is at my right hand, I shall not be moved. Therefore my heart is glad...my flesh also shall rest in hope. Psalm 16:5–9

Trust in the LORD, and do good...Delight yourself also in the LORD; and he shall give you the desires of your heart. Commit your ways to the LORD; trust also in him; and he shall bring it to pass. Rest in the LORD.... Psalm 37:3–7

...you shall be like a watered garden, and like a spring of water, whose waters fail not. Isaiah 58:11

Jesus; Lord of LORDS: Come to me, all you who labour and are heavy laden, and I will give you rest. Take my yoke upon you, and learn of me; for I am meek and lowly in heart: and you shall find rest for your souls. For my yoke is easy, and my burden is light.
Matthew 11:28–30

Let us therefore fear, lest, a promise being left us of entering into his rest, any of you should seem to come short of it...For we which have believed do enter into rest...There remains therefore a rest to the people of God. For he that enters into his rest, he also has ceased from his own works, as God did from his. Let us labour therefore to enter into that rest.... Hebrews 4:1–11

Jesus said: "The sabbath was made for man, and not man for the sabbath." Mark 2:27

4
The LORD God

These are the generations of the heavens and of the earth when they were created, in the day that the LORD God made the earth and the heavens.
And every plant of the field before it was in the earth, and every herb of the field before it grew: for the LORD God had not caused it to rain upon the earth, and there was not a man to till the ground.
But there went up a mist from the earth, and watered the whole face of the ground.

Genesis 2:4–6

BIBLICAL scholars believe that two different authors wrote the first two chapters of Genesis because of the change in the writing style. Maybe, maybe not.

In the first chapter and into chapter 2:3, only God is mentioned as creating the heaven and the earth because the heaven of heavens (the heaven with no s) and the earth (the cosmos) were created from God the Energy and the Light.

Heaven was created first from energy forces that we are not familiar with, and before the earth ever was. The span of time between heaven and earth in the first verse is beyond human comprehension. In the realm of the everlasting, time does not exist.

Now in Genesis 2:4, no more is said about the third heaven, and the creation story goes on to tell about the *heavens* and the earth.

> *"These are the generations of the heavens [with an s] and the earth when they were created, in the day that the LORD God made the earth and the heavens."*

The word *earth* in the Bible is the cosmos that is within the universe (the universe was not created—it always was); it is the general term for all that is matter, or dust. Earth is also the dry ground of the cosmos that the sons of men inhabit. In this particular verse, it is referring to our fragment of earth and the rest of the cosmos that are the heavens.

(I know I have explained most of this before, but I will repeat some of these very important details because they are key to understanding the Bible's mysteries.)

It took generations, or—in God's time—one day, for the LORD God to *make* the cosmos out of the elements of matter that were *created* from the Energy of God.

The LORD in this verse is the embodiment of the Creator, the first to be created, the LORD of all the LORDS in heaven and the only begotten Son of God. In essence he is God, but he is lower in status than God. Therefore, he is the LORD God, for he made all the worlds.

> For God so loved the world, that he gave his only begotten Son... .
> John 3:16

> ...whom he has appointed heir of all things, by whom also he made the worlds; Hebrews 1:2

> Jesus prayed to God: And now, O Father, glorify me with your own self with the glory which I had with you before the world was.
> John 17:5

> I [Jesus] am Alpha and Omega, the beginning and the end, the first and the last. Revelation 22:13

> Who has wrought and done it, calling the generations from the beginning? I the LORD, the first, and with the last; I am he.
> Isaiah 41:4

> For thus says the LORD that created the heavens; God himself that formed the earth and made it; he has established it, he created it not in vain, he formed it to be inhabited: I am the LORD and there is none else. Isaiah 45:18

In the New Testament of English Bibles, and in all other literature of Christian origin, the title *Lord* (with only the letter *L* uppercase) refers to Jesus.

In the Old Testament of the Christian English Bibles, the title is sometimes written *LORD* (all letters uppercase). The LORD or the LORD GOD (today we would say LORD of GOD) was either the Son of God (who was yet to come), one of the LORDS of heaven, or a LORD from another planet (who the people of the time may have thought was from heaven since he came from the sky). The context it is in makes it clear as to whom it refers.

Bible dictionaries define *LORD* or *Lord* as an abbreviation for Jehovah, who they believe is another name for God. No! Jehovah is NOT God. The word *LORD* or *Lord* is a title given to someone to take the place of someone of higher rank; to act in his place, and speak for him and as he would speak. It is a title, not a nickname.

When *God* is used alone it means the Almighty, the Creator and the Supreme Being. When *our God* is used in a passage it means that the LORD is the God of a particular people or nation and not necessarily the God of everyone. Jehovah was the God of the Israelites and a Lord from the heaven of heavens.

> Trust in the LORD forever: for in the LORD JEHOVAH is everlasting strength Isaiah 26:4

In the Old Testament, a *Lord* was a man of high rank from this planet. Sometimes he was a prince of a nation, but mostly he was a prophet or patriarch of his people and he would refer to himself as *lord* (no uppercase) or call himself *a servant of the LORD* or *a servant of God.*

The people generally honored prophets, and even the elders, the princes and kings held them in high esteem because they were the intermediaries between the people and the LORD of heaven, whom they could not see or hear. A prophet could interpret his dreams and visions and could presumably hear the voice of the LORD, and he would then pass on the message.

Even a LORD of the sky (from another planet) was seldom accessible to the common folk, and appeared to communicate with only a select few, such as a patriarch or an intelligent and educated king. For the people, the prophet was as close as they could get to a God. They could see him, touch him and hear him speak—he was their Lord.

> The word of the LORD came again to me, saying, Son of man, say to the prince of Tyrus, Thus says the Lord God [the Lord of God]...
> .
> Ezekiel 28:1 – 2

In the book of Daniel, Daniel confesses to the transgressions of the Israelites and asks the LORD God to forgive them. They had their Lord Jeremiah at the time, but they did not listen to him, and rebelled against him:

> Neither have we hearkened unto your servants, the prophets, which spoke in your name to our kings, our princes, and our fathers, and to all the people of the land." Daniel 9:6

Through prayer to the LORD God again, he speaks directly to the Lord Jeremiah (who has passed on) and tells him that the people don't really deserve his forgiveness: "to us belongs confusion of face...because we have sinned against you." (Daniel 9:8)

Then he goes on to beg for mercy for the Lord God Jeremiah, from the LORD of heaven. The prophet did try to be a good servant, but the people were a hindrance: "To the Lord our God belong mercies and forgivenesses, though we have rebelled against him" (Daniel 9:9)

> I beseech you, O LORD God of heaven, the great and terrible God, that keeps covenant and mercy for them that love him and observe his commandments. Nehemiah 1:5

The LORD God of heaven, appointed to watch over and guide this primitive nation on this still young planet, had to set down rules, regulations, covenants and commandments, much like parents with a family of children. They were dealing with the infancy of humankind.

The average person did not have the abstract thought that was necessary to fully comprehend the laws of nature or its catastrophes, such as floods, volcanic eruptions or earthquakes, and most could not understand the laws of cause and effect: "what you sow so shall you reap." Like flocks of sheep, they needed their shepherds.

They did not, however, always listen to their prophet, the Lord, when he tried to intervene and warn them of the consequences of their actions. If something went wrong, it was the LORD in heaven who punished them with flood, famine or, sometimes, the sword of another nation.

Thus, the Old Testament is full of the sins of the people, an angry LORD God and, at times, a Lord who didn't always get the message across in the way he would have liked.

> O LORD our God, other lords besides you have had dominion over us: But by you only will we make mention of your name. They are dead, they shall not live; they are deceased, they shall not rise. . . .
>
> Isaiah 26:13 – 14

> Wherefore David blessed the LORD. . . and David said, Blessed be thou, LORD God of Israel our father. . . yours is the kingdom, O LORD, and you are exalted as head above all. Now therefore, our God, we thank you, and praise your glorious name. 1 Chronicles 29:10 – 13

In this passage, "David blessed the LORD." People do not bless God. Therefore this LORD is not God. People ask for God's blessing for themselves or for someone else who was created by God, such as a LORD.

"and you are exalted as head above all." To be exalted means to be elevated in rank. Who would elevate the Creator? This LORD was given the rank to be above all other LORDS over the nation of Israel.

David, in one of his prophetic psalms, speaks of the LORD, the Son of God who will one day in the future of David's era come down to this planet. He will come as a male child born of a woman from his people and he will teach this world how to live the kingdom of heaven on earth. For a brief moment in time, from his message to his physical death, the LORD of LORDS and the host of heaven will lower himself to be a Lord among his earthly brothers and sisters. He will become a *Son of men*!

> O LORD our Lord, how excellent is your name in all the earth! who has set your glory above the heavens. Out of the mouth of babes and sucklings have you ordained strength because of your enemies, that you might still the enemy and the avenger. When I consider your heavens, the work of your fingers, the moon and the stars, which you have ordained; What is man, that you are mindful of him? and the son of man, that you visit him? For you have made him a little lower than the angels, and have crowned him with glory and honour. You made him to have dominion over the works of your hands; you have put all things under his feet: All sheep and oxen, yea, and the beasts of the field; The fowl of the air, and the fish of the sea, and whatsoever passes through the paths of the seas. O LORD our Lord, how excellent is your name in all the earth!
>
> Psalm 8

ooo

"These are the generations...in the day that the LORD God made the earth and the heavens, And every plant of the field before it was in the earth, and every herb of the field before it grew: for the LORD God had not caused it to rain upon the earth...But there went up a mist from the earth, and watered the whole face of the ground."

The emphasis in Genesis 2:4 – 6 is that nothing was created in an instant. The Son of God created and made the heavens and the earth that is the cosmos. Then, from the cosmos, our little blue globe that had been one of those flung out from the molten rock was now forming and developing into a world of life. It had no atmosphere as yet that could bring on the rain, but then it didn't need the rain because nothing was alive. There were no plants, no animals and no people. It was the dawn of the third day.

> *"But there went up a mist from the earth which watered the whole face of the ground."*

> He hangs the earth upon nothing. . . and binds up the waters in his thick clouds; and the cloud is not rent under them. Job 26:7 – 8

This rocky globe, saturated with internal steaming water, was slowly cooling down, and there went up a mist and formed a thick cloud. It was being made ready for the properties of life.

Just as with the conception and growth of a child in the womb and then the birth of that child, so the inhospitable flint cast off from the flaming stars had to become a womb of moisture and warmth for the birth and growth of life.

The various gases culminating under the thick blanket of cloud and the dissolving minerals in the rocks would, in eons of time, bring together the elements conducive to the molecules of life.

Then on the eve of the third day, Mother Earth brought forth the germs of life; first came the grasses, then the herbs of the field and, finally, the stately trees. After many more eons, she gave birth to the moving creature that has life; that her waters brought forth, male and female, after its kind. And God saw that it was all very good.

These were the generations of evolution made by *the LORD God* who was the *Son of God*.

5
The Potter and The Clay

And the LORD God formed man of the dust of the ground, and breathed into his nostrils the breath of life; and man became a living soul.

Genesis 2:7

EVERYTHING had been *created* and *made* by God and the Son of God. It was finished, and evolving according to the Almighty plan. There were male and female in plant and animal; they were multiplying and were fruitful, and were replenishing the earth into the generations.

During the eons of the sixth day, the various kinds of mammals evolved from the moving creatures from the waters of an earlier time. Among these mammals was an animal we know today as a primate, and one of the species of primate was called *man*: an animal destined to rule over all the others and have dominion over all of the earth.

On the evening of the sixth day of creation, God said *in thought* to his LORD of LORDS and the LORDS of heaven, "Let us make *man* in *our* image...male and female...."

And man, one of the species of primate, evolved into several different kinds of hominids over the millennia.

Although man had been blessed with a higher profile, he was still within the animal kingdom and subject to the laws of nature. Some species grew and multiplied and some died out, as is the way of all life on earth. Several of these hominid types developed a larger brain and a more agile thumb than their primate cousins and would, in the process of time, learn to speak, think in symbols, and make tools for survival.

Paleoanthropologists, over the years, have unearthed many fossils in various stages of hominid evolution, some dating back three million years. In recent years, the skull of a child was discovered in a deep, sediment-filled cave in northern Spain. The child, along with the bones of other children and animals, had been the victim of cannibalism judging by the way the bones had been scraped and cut by a sharp object. What was so peculiar about this particular skull was that the teeth were Neanderthal and the jaw resembled an even earlier type of hominid, but as the scientists excitedly exclaimed, "the face was ours." And yet, according to the carbon dating, this child, along with its peers, had lain in the cave for 800,000 years.

Some scientists believe that at one point in our ancient prehistory at least three different species of hominids lived at the same time and in the same areas, and may even have interbred. They were the Homo erectus, the Neanderthal, and the near-modern Homo sapien, and it could have been as late as 35,000 years ago. The dates are still hotly debated, as is the proposed coexistence of the different hominid groups.

From this latest discovery of the *Homo antecessor* (what this new group is called), it is believed that some humans appeared almost modern 800,000 years ago, and perhaps even earlier than that.

o o o

The planet had cooled and the heavy cloud enveloping it had dispersed. Eons had passed. The grasses, the herbs and the trees covered the ground with a carpet of green, and animals and hominids were well into their evolutionary life spans. More time passed—eons and eons of time. Then, as a poet of the Dead Sea Scrolls related, ancient things were removed and new things were created "by breaking asunder things anciently established, and raising up the things of eternity."

The various species of hominids would eventually die out and become extinct, as did many other plants and animals, and new life would rise from the old. From the primitive hominids, the LORD God formed a man—one man—"of the dust of the ground," and called his name *Adam*.

ADAM—THE FIRST MODERN HOMO SAPIEN! THE MISSING LINK!

Adam was not the first human to be born on this planet (yes, he was born). There were already many people (we call them *hominids*) in the world, and they had probably spread throughout the African and Eurasian continents. As we know, there were many types of hominids, and in various stages of development, but none were modern, or completely Homo sapien.

In the Bible, when God first ordained the species called *man* to have dominion over the earth, he was named then, and throughout the Bible, as the *son of man* or the *sons of men.*

The LORD of LORDS is the Son of God (uppercase *S*) *and* he is also the Son of man (uppercase *S*).

We are the sons of men (lowercase *s*).

When the LORD God formed Adam, the first Homo sapien, he also became the *son of God* (lowercase *s*).

"And the LORD God formed man of the dust of the ground. . . ."

Bible readers have always pictured God crouched beside the riverbank molding a full-grown man from a pack of wet clay.

Let's get real!

First: God is Energy and Light; he has no shape or form—he is Conscious Energy. He is through all and in all and above all. If God had physically come down and formed Adam, he would have disintegrated the poor guy before he'd have gotten any breath into him.

No one can see God and live!

Second: It was not the LORD God of heaven who came down to our planet and formed Adam. As I have mentioned before, the Bible does not distinguish between the LORDS of heaven and the LORDS of the heavens (men from other worlds) except in the verse or passage that explains their duty or the role they play.

Some religious literature of Jewish origin says the LORD Jehovah was the LORD that came down and formed Adam, and it could very well be that it was the LORD in heaven who instigated the making of the first modern man: the "missing link."

The LORD Jehovah in heaven would have worked through his servant, the LORD God from the sky, because the LORDS of heaven are spirits and they do not come down to the earth. They communicate to humans through the angels, through dreams and visions, and through the process of thought.

Third: The LORD *of* God who made Adam was a highly evolved person from a distant world in the universe and his planet could have been thousands, or even millions, of years ahead of ours. Maybe through communication with the LORD Jehovah, he and his team set up residence here for awhile to modernize the hominid of this planet and make him "in our image and our likeness."

Long after the Adamic race was made, people and nations around the world knew of, and were visited by, those from other worlds. The Semitic tribes referred to them as LORDS and, sometimes, angels or messengers from God. Other nations, such as Egypt, Greece and Rome, called them *gods*, and their accounts come down to us as legends and myths inspired by vivid imaginations.

These LORDS and gods were different from the LORDS of heaven; they were made of flesh and blood and they could mingle with the sons of men. There were gods and goddesses, and they sometimes had sons and daughters, and they could be benevolent or malevolent—whatever they felt like being. They were loved and feared and they were worshipped and appeased with offerings, sacrifices, and gifts. These gods and LORD gods came from the skies and went back up into the skies in "flaming chariots that had eyes round about and thundered with the voice of God."

> O LORD, our God, other lords besides you have had dominion over us...but they are dead...they are deceased... .
>
> Isaiah 26:13–14

When our planet was just beginning to be a world it must have been a real attraction for the more advanced worlds in the cosmos, just as we would be if we found a new planet with primitive life on it. The intellectual, the spiritual and the curious visited our world; some were gods, some were LORD Gods who deserved the title, and some were jerks that came along for the ride. Perhaps someday, we too will send our scientists and our spiritual advisors, and maybe even some jerks, to an unsuspecting planet.

Fourth: The name of this particular LORD God who made Adam was not given, as was the custom of the biblical scribes. He came and worked under the spiritual guidance of the LORD God of heaven who is said to have been Jehovah. It is the LORD God of heaven who is credited with the creation of the new man because the earthly LORDS and Lords are only the servants, as were the prophets of old.

Today we would say that this LORD was a scientist or a doctor, and he was likely an expert in the field of genetic engineering and cell manipulation. He and his team came (all scientists have a team) or were sent by a higher authority to speed up the slow and haphazard process of hominid evolution.

The hominids that existed were in various stages of development and they had *rough edges* that needed to be *toned down* or eliminated from the human body of the future and to be in the likeness and image of those from more advanced nations of the cosmos. A brighter looking, more intellectual and more attractive man was needed.

After selecting the preferred characteristics from the available gene pool, an embryo was implanted into the womb of a specially chosen female who may or may not have been Adam's biological mother; she could have been a surrogate mother from the LORD'S team. The Bible doesn't say who the woman was, but in keeping with the laws of Mother Nature, all life on earth begins as an embryo. Even the Son of God, when he became a Son of man for a short stay on this planet, had to start out as an embryo born of an earthly woman, and Adam was no different in this respect.

Yes, Adam had a belly button. He may have been conceived in a petri dish, but he had a mother who nursed him and cuddled him during his infancy and there may even have been several parental figures within this compound of scientists to assist in raising Adam to manhood.

Dad might have been a conglomerate of whoever and whatever, but there is the possibility also that Adam's father was this LORD God from a more advanced planet because it was the LORD God who would later place Adam into a garden and teach him how to be *one of them*.

Adam was different from the hominids outside of the small community of space people; he was more perfect in body and mind, and, while the others were still in the animal kingdom, he was a *son of God*.

The Bible emphasizes that "the LORD God formed man of the dust of the ground. . . ." The Bible refers to *all* that is in the cosmos as dust; all that is matter is dust and all that is dust is Earth. Adam, like the rest of the life on this planet, came from the dust of the ground when the earth brought forth the living creature after his kind. His ancestors were the various hominid races, the primates before them, and the mammals after their kind and after the moving creature that came from the waters.

We *are* all ONE.

> *"And he breathed into his nostrils the breath of life; and man became a living soul."*

All physical life has to breathe in order to live. Life begins with a breath—it is called *birth*. Before birth, it is the mother that breathes and at birth there is a breath and a *soul* is born. With the last breath the soul leaves, and the physical garment returns to the dust from which it came.

Adam was formed of the dust of the earth, as was all terrestrial life, and when he was born he took his first breath of the life that "the Spirit of God moved upon the face of the waters." And this first Homo sapien on this planet became a *living soul*. This meant that Adam, unlike the hominids and animals, had a soul that could learn of the Kingdom of God within him, be capable of wisdom beyond knowledge, and be a "son of God" in God's image and likeness.

> Thus says the LORD that made you, and formed you from the womb. . . .
> Isaiah 44:2

NEOTENY: The retention of the adult in a species, of juvenile characteristics of an ancestor.

As I have mentioned, the hominids around and about at the time must still have had some rough edges in their anatomy and facial features that needed to be toned down.

Neoteny can occur naturally through evolution, as we have found fossils of animals that became either shorter or taller and more refined in features as time went on.

Over the centuries, humankind has assisted nature in the process of neoteny by domesticating some animals and plants so they barely resemble their wild ancestors. Notice, for example, the wild boar compared to the domestic pig on the farm, or the mountain goats and sheep compared to the goats and sheep in the pasture. To domesticate is to coddle, protect, look after and feed on demand, and to interbreed with similar qualities.

In the 1920's, a Dutch anatomist, Louis Bolk, had already thought that the modern human had been altered in some way through a natural occurrence in the evolutionary process. He thought that essentially we are "retarded apes."

Through the science of neoteny, the LORD doctor would have made Adam more slender in facial features and bone structure and a little taller with a more upright stance to result in a more youthful appearance.

Adam had a new appearance: he was kept away from *the herd* and he was coddled in a fruitful and peaceful garden with all of his needs met, and he was taught to be a "son of God."

> Then I (Jeremiah) went down to the potter's house, and, behold, he wrought a work on the wheels. And the vessel that he made of clay was marred in the hand of the potter: so he made it again another vessel, as seemed good to the potter to make it...as the clay is in the potter's hand, so are you in my hand.... Jeremiah 18:3–6

> O LORD, you are our father; we are the clay, and you our potter; and we all are the work of your hand. Isaiah 64:8

(Notice in this verse that Isaiah refers to the LORD as "father" with a lowercase *f*. This is further proof that this LORD was not God who is *always* Father capitalized.)

The Y Chromosome

In 1995, Michael Hammer, a research scientist at the University of Arizona, published an article in the journal *Nature* of his work on the Y chromosome. In his findings, he discovered that every man on earth (this planet) could trace his Y chromosome back to one male about 190,000 years ago.

He went on to say that there were many males around at the time, but that they weren't as anatomically modern as humans are today. Of all the different species of hominids, it appears that only this one man left a Y chromosome legacy that persists today. The Y chromosome is the only one of 24 types that is passed down only from father to son.

This also supports the theory that modern humans developed in just one place on the map. As Hammer said, "We would all have the same Y chromosome that existed in the same guy."

He went on to say that his study suggests that modern humans came from a small breeding group over the last 200,000 years. "The group was so small that it's hard to believe its members could have spread out over more than one continent."

In the Bible, this small group was known as the *sons of God*, a modern species of the sons of men—the Adamic race.

> ...what manner of love the Father has bestowed upon us, that we should be called the sons of God.... 1 John 3:1

> Jesus...being the son of Joseph...which was the son of David...which was the son of Abraham...which was the son of Seth...which was the son of Adam, which was the son of God.
> Luke 3:23–38

> Even everyone that is called by my name: for I have created him for my glory, I have formed him; yea, I have made him.
> Isaiah 43:7

Adam was destined and *designed* to be the father and patriarch of a new and modern species of humans on this planet and to begin a New World Order. He would be domesticated, protected and, for a time, separated from those on the outside. He didn't look like them, he was physically and mentally superior, and within a garden setting he would thrive in mind, consciousness and soul.

The LORD God, Adam's guardian, and his team were of the most intelligent of earthly beings and they would teach the young Adam everything he needed to know about the God of heaven and earth, and how to live the *rest* that was ordained for all creation. Adam was placed in a garden paradise to show him how life was to be, and he was to enlighten his descendants about the kingdom of heaven within and how to recreate a paradise on earth in the mirror image of the one in heaven.

6
The Garden of Eden

And the LORD God planted a garden eastward in Eden; and there he put the man whom he had formed.
And out of the ground made the LORD God to grow every tree that is pleasant to the sight, and good for food; the tree of life also in the midst of the garden, and the tree of knowledge of good and evil.
And a river went out of Eden to water the garden; and from there it was parted, and became into four heads.
The name of the first is Pison: that is it which compasses the whole land of Havilah, where there is gold;
And the gold of that land is good: there is bdellium (gum resin) and the onyx stone (Beryl stone).
And the name of the second river is Gihon: the same is it that compasses the whole land of Ethiopia.
And the name of the third river is Hiddekel (Tigris) that is it which goes toward the east of Assyria. And the fourth river is Euphrates.

Genesis 2:8–14

DR. JURIS ZARINS of Southwest Missouri State University came to the conclusion that the garden of Eden now lies beneath the waters of the Persian Gulf.[1]

There was a time, thousands of years ago during the Great Ice Age, when the Persian Gulf was dry land, as were most regions of the planet. When the ice melted, many rivers and streams became swollen into lakes and gulfs, and some dry land became part of the ocean.

Geological investigations have revealed that two gullies known today as the Wadi Rimah and the Wadi Batin were once ancient rivers and the remains of the Pison, and the Gihon is the Karun River of the present time. The Pison River that encompassed the whole land of Havilah is that which, in Genesis 25:18, is "before Egypt, as you go toward Assyria."

The garden was planted *east* of Eden. Eden was the biblical name of the land that later was called *Mesopotamia*, west of the Persian Gulf and what is now Iraq. East of Eden would place the garden in the Persian Gulf.

The valley west of the Gulf was fertile, and the climate was neither too hot nor too cool. It was watered by four rivers that would make it into a lush paradise with trees of every kind, and the region around it was rich in the minerals and precious gems that would put a glint in the eye of the future Homosapien. Thousands of animal bones and stone tools have been found in the area, and this is evidence of a once well- populated human habitation.

Scientists believe that the hominid originated in Africa, and that could well be, but Homo sapien was the newest and latest model and he appeared much later, and long after the various species of hominids had already wandered off into Europe and Asia.

Although all the life forms of plant and animal had spread over the globe and replenished the earth, this fertile valley of Eden was chosen above all others to be the cradle of civilization for this planet.

The King James Bible gives us an accurate map of the region where the garden was located. It was probably very much like the closed-in parks and natural reserves that we have today, and it was designed for beauty, fresh fruit, and peace and tranquillity. It was also to be a microcosm of a paradise on earth where the sons of God would learn of the cosmic union of body and soul, of the life of *rest*, and of the kingdom of heaven that was within them.

In Hebrew, Eden means *luxury, pleasure, delight*. The Sumerian word *Edin* means a *plain steppe*, and a Sumerian myth tells of a land that once existed where age, sickness and death were unknown to its fortunate inhabitants.

Many ancient cultures had legends of an earlier time when humankind lived free from fear and pain, and when there were as yet no snakes or scorpions and no thorns or briers. The legends were passed down through the ages and embellished with sentimentality, and whether it was the garden of Eden or the Shangri-La of the Himalayas, it was something that humans feel they once had and is now lost forever—a faded memory buried deep in the subconscious mind.

In the *Tehi*, one of the oldest writings found in China, it states that in the beginning of ancient times China was ruled for 18,000 years by a race of Divine Kings. It was an age of peace and contentment for both humans and animals and "body and soul were in cosmic union." They lived in a garden setting, and crime was unknown.[2]

The fables come from all parts of the world and are similar in the telling—it was the perfect existence, without crime or sorrow, and the people either originated from the stars or were ruled by someone who came from the stars.

In *The Book of the Dead*[3], Khnemu was one of the gods from the sky who helped in the creation of the universe, and it was he who fashioned the first man on the potter's wheel (it was a unique procedure and unlike that of the rest of creation). Although the early Egyptians had many beliefs in their religions that were surprisingly similar to biblical accounts, it doesn't appear as though they had a garden of paradise or an age of perfection as some others had.

The Bible does not say when the garden of Eden existed, but even if a date were given, it would be of little value to us. In the book of Genesis many of the early patriarchs' ages were given when they *begat* so and so, and how old they were when they died. Adam was said to have lived 930 years, and Methuselah, supposedly the oldest man to have ever lived, was 969 years when he died.

Before recorded history we have no way of knowing how these early people and their societies measured time, or if they even had a set method of dating in months and years. We do not know how long a year was in Adam's time or if it was calculated from the movements of the sun, the moon or the stars—or any of these. It is thought that some tribes measured time by the seasons, by following migrating animals for hunting, or by the time they planted crops; but in some parts of the world crops can be planted two or even three times within a season. That still doesn't give us an answer as to how time was measured before the development of agriculture.

When the planet was still very young it was spinning a little faster than now; we have slowed down somewhat. That would have made a year, or an agricultural season, shorter than the present time and a faster spinning planet could partially explain the longevity of the people in Adam's day.

Adam was still *begetting* sons and daughters at the tender age of 130 years, and Methuselah was 187 years old when he had another son. These old boys did not need Viagra! Granted, the air was pure and the fruit and veggies came straight from a very fertile soil. That is not saying, however, that everyone lived to these ripe old ages. Only the patriarchs are mentioned.

Research scientist Michael Hammer's Y chromosome discovery traces the modern Homo sapien back almost 200,000 years and, to me, that seems like a logical time for Adam to have been born and the garden of Eden to have been planted.

ooo

Together with his staff, the LORD God set up his residence and laboratory in the land of Eden, and when Adam was born into the world the LORD God became his physical and spiritual guardian.

Undoubtedly Adam would have been a typical child: he would have had his playtime and there would have been tears, temper tantrums, and broken toys; but in this well-adjusted environment Adam would have been highly educated and given guidance on acceptable and unacceptable behavior. As Adam grew into a responsible and good person in the physical realm, he would then leave his nursery in Eden and continue his spiritual learning in the garden of Eden.

"And the LORD God planted a garden. . . ."

In Genesis 2:4–6 the LORD God *made* the heavens and the earth from that which was *created* from God the Energy and the Light. That LORD God was the LORD of LORDS, the Son of God.

The LORD God of Eden, as I mentioned earlier, was not the same LORD God in Genesis 2:4–6. The LORD God who *formed* Adam was a man of the earth and from one of the many waters in the universe. He did not create a man and he did not create or make a garden by saying, "Let it be" or "let it come forth." He PLANTED a garden east of Eden and *out of the ground* he made to *grow* every tree.

In the midst of the garden of trees that were pleasant to the sight and good for food were the metaphoric *tree of life* and the *tree of knowledge of good and evil.*

The Tree of Life

The garden was planted by the LORD God and grew with the blessing of Mother Nature. The trees of life and the knowledge of good and evil were not real trees; they were METAPHORS.

An earthly garden can be described by any writer and can be envisioned in the mind of any reader—beautiful trees, flowers and sparkling rivers with tumbling waterfalls, but how does one describe mind, consciousness and soul?

This garden was planted not only for its physical and material nourishment, but also for the subsistence and nourishment of the newly formed human—made in "our image and likeness" as a spirit from the Spirit. It was a sanctuary to preserve a species, a species whose brain was superior to any other animal or hominid on the planet and could, with that brain, know the Creator and have dominion over his creation with wisdom and intelligence.

Besides being a sanctuary, the garden of Eden was, most of all, a learning center, a school in how to be a *son of God* and awaken the *living soul* that is in the body made of clay.

> To him that overcomes will I give to eat of the tree of life, which is in the midst of the paradise of God.... Revelation 2:7

> Happy is the man that finds wisdom, and the man that gets understanding...it is better than silver...and the gain thereof than fine gold. She is more precious than rubies: and all the things that you desire are not to be compared to her. Length of days is in her right hand, and in her left hand riches and honour. Her ways are ways of pleasantness, and all her paths are peace. She [wisdom] is the tree of life to them that lay hold upon her: and happy is every one that retains her...the wise shall inherit glory: but shame shall be the promotion of fools. Proverbs 3:13–35

In Ode 42 in the book of *Solomon* (not in the Bible), he prophesied of the coming of the Son of God as "stretching my hands as spread on a tree."[4]

When Jesus died on the cross (which had been a tree) with his arms spread out, it was God's sign of the tree of life. Jesus came to teach us the wisdom and mysteries of God. He was, and is, the tree of life.

In one of the earliest and badly deteriorated hieroglyphics are found these words:

He has eaten the knowledge of God every, [his] existence eternity....

Deceased asks the god Anu: "How long have I to live?"

Answer: "You shall exist for millions of millions of years...soul to heaven body to earth."[5]

The Tree of the Knowledge of Good and Evil

Just as the tree of life was a spiritual tree pertaining to the wisdom of God for the human soul, the tree of knowledge of good and evil relates to the psychology of the human brain.

We are spirits clothed in matter. We live in a cosmos made of matter and we were given dominion over all that is made of matter. All matter is subject to certain laws that we call "the laws of nature," and to keep nature healthy and happy we must stay within the law. This is called *ecology*. We have dominion, but dominion does not mean exploitation. It means that we are to be sovereigns and to look after all that is ours: our bodies and our world.

All matter has body and is dimensional—length and width, inside and outside, up and down, front and back. There is substance and there is lack of substance, there are parallels and there are opposites. All of these constitute our physicality. In our psychological constitution, we also have the dimension of opposites, and substance and lack of substance.

Unlike the rest of the animal kingdom, we can choose how we want to live, and we have the knowledge of good and evil. To do good is to abide by the laws of God and nature, and to do evil is to break the law. In the Bible it is called a *sin*.

Maimonides, a Jewish philosopher of the Middle Ages, described the concept of evil and wrote of the paradox of the existence of evil in a universe created by a God of all mercy and all justice:

> Evil is not a thing, but a non-thing; it is the absence of good. (A parallel in the physical world would be a definition of cold as the absence of heat.) Evil is made possible by the imperfection of matter; this lack does not permit matter, animate and inanimate, to receive

> or to perceive the divine good. However, since evil does exist in God's creation, it also has a positive aspect; it serves some good purpose. For example, sickness and death are evils, but they are also necessary in a finite universe peopled with finite beings. The very process of continuing creation requires these evils; creation is birth and growth, which imply decay and death.

Maimonides went on to say that there are three types or qualities of evil:

> The evil caused by nature (storms, earthquakes, or drought), the evil caused by one man to another (war and violence), and the evil man does to himself...There are two kinds of divine providence: that extended to man, and that extended to all other living things...The providence extended to man...is directed to each individual, who is then left free to follow God's providence or not.[6]

Although evolution strives for perfection in a cosmos of matter, nature is not perfect and cannot be perfect because it has to evolve continually. It cannot be idle and stop its movement. It has its dimensions and its opposing forces that we are inclined to call good and evil, but is an earthquake evil, or a storm, or a flood?

We think of viruses, germs and bacteria as dangerous and evil, but they also give us health and we cannot live without them. It is a matter of what is where, and at what time. A beautiful and productive plant can be a weed in the wrong area of the garden, and thorns and briers have their place in the family of plants, as do snakes and scorpions in the animal kingdom.

We accept the evils of nature, somewhat, because most of it is beyond our control, but we do have, and must have, control over the good and evil actions of our own species. We are the only beings in the world of living creatures that have the tree of knowledge of good and evil in our midst. No other animal in the world or in the universe has that knowledge.

Animals strive for comfort and contentment, and all have within them the instinct for survival, regardless of what it takes. And no matter what it takes, they cannot commit evil, and they cannot sin; not even our hominid ancestors were capable of being evil or sinning, as they were still within the animal kingdom. Only our species, throughout the cosmos, has that knowledge inherited from God. It is the God in us. We have dominion and only we, above all earthly creatures, have a *choice* as to what we do with that knowledge. We can destroy our world and ourselves or we can be the sons of God and make our planet into a paradise on earth.

The choice is ours and ours alone.

> Therefore all things whatsoever you would that men should do to you, do even so to them: for this is the law and the prophets.
>
> Matthew 7:12

> Keep your tongue from evil, and your lips from speaking guile. Depart from evil and do good; seek peace, and pursue it. . . .
>
> Psalm 34:13 – 14

> These does the LORD hate. . .a proud look, a lying tongue and hands that shed innocent blood. . .a heart that devises wicked imaginations, feet that be swift in running to mischief. A false witness that speaks lies, and he that sows discord among brethren. . . .
>
> Proverbs 6:16 – 19

> A wise man fears, and departs from evil: but the fool rages, and is confident. . .He that is soon angry deals foolishly. . .He that is slow to wrath is of great understanding. . .A sound heart is the life of the flesh: but envy the rottenness of the bones. He that oppresses the poor reproaches his Maker: but he that honours him has mercy on the poor. . .Righteousness exalts a nation: but sin is a reproach to any people. . .
>
> Proverbs 14:16 – 34

> Though I speak with the tongues of men and of angels, and have not charity, I am become as sounding brass, or a tinkling cymbal. . .Charity suffers long, and is kind; charity envies not; charity does not boast of itself, is not puffed up. Does not behave itself unseemly. . .is not easily provoked, thinks no evil. . . .
>
> 1 Corinthians 13:1 – 5

> Whatsoever things are true, whatsoever things are honest, whatsoever things are just, whatsoever things are pure, whatsoever things are lovely, whatsoever things are of good report; if they be any virtue, and if there be any praise, think on these things…and the God of peace shall be with you. Philippians 4:8 – 9

NOTES

[1] The Reader's Digest Association, Inc. (1988). *Readers Digest "Mysteries of the Bible".* Pleasantville, NY: The Reader's Digest Association, Inc., p. 24

[2] Drake, W.R. (1968). *Gods and Spacemen in the Ancient East.* Scarborough, ON: New American Library of Canada, p. 85.

[3] Budge, E.A.W. (1960). *The Book of the Dead.* New York, NY: University Books, p. 173.

[4] Barnstone, W. (1984). *The Other Bible.* New York, NY: HarperCollins, p. 284.

[5] Budge, E.A.W. (1960). *The Book of the Dead.* New York, NY: University Books, p. 67.

[6] Gersh, H. (1968). *The Sacred Book of the Jews.* New York, NY: Stein and Day Publishers, p. 193–94.

7
Adam's Rib

And the LORD God took the man, and put him into the garden of Eden to dress it and to keep it.
And the LORD God commanded the man, saying, Of every tree of the garden you may freely eat:
But of the tree of the knowledge of good and evil, you shall not eat of it: for in the day that you eat thereof you shall surely die.
Genesis 2:15 – 17

THE first man of a new species was put into the garden "to dress it and to keep it." The garden of Eden was a microcosm of our watery-blue globe, and we, the progenies of this man, are here to dress it and to keep it. It is our duty. We owe it to our Creator, and to ourselves, to be good stewards and look after the world and its many creatures with the humanity and intelligence that we were originally endowed with. At last report, we haven't been doing so well.

Adam was different from his fellow hominids outside the LORD'S compound in Eden. He was made from them, but he was physically, mentally and spiritually superior to them.

The hominids did what they had to do to survive and, like the rest of the animal kingdom that they were still a part of, it was survival of the fittest. They did not know right from wrong, nor did they have the knowledge of good and evil. In the process of evolution they were the beginning of the *sons of men*, and over the millennia they would *all* become extinct.

From Adam, our species of human is equal in status to those far off among the stars and the many waters. In the Bible, Adam and his generations were called the *sons of God* to differentiate them from the *sons of men*.

As time went on, perhaps when there were no more hominid species and when the sons of God were "only evil continually," the Bible began to refer to *all* of humanity as the *sons of men*. Only on occasion in the Old Testament, as in the book of Job, was any reference made to the *sons of God*.

In the New Testament, anyone who followed the teachings of Jesus and became a convert would once again be a son of God.

I will repeat what I have said in Chapter Five—the *sons of God* in the Bible are NOT angels. Despite what biblical scholars and Bible dictionaries have stated, there is not any place anywhere that refers to angels as the *sons of God*.

> (Jesus)…Being made so much better than the angels…For unto which of the angels said he at any time, You are my Son, this day have I begotten you…But to which of the angels said he at any time, Sit on my right hand, until I make your enemies your footstool? Are they not all ministering spirits, sent forth to minister for them who shall be heirs of salvation? Hebrews 1:4–14

We are lower than angels. They are ministering spirits for us and we are the heirs of salvation, but only if we choose to be. If we choose to do only good then we will, once again, be referred to as the *sons of God*.

When Adam moved into the garden of Eden, he was warned about the tree of the knowledge of good and evil. Here we see the paternal instincts come to the surface in the LORD God. All during Adam's childhood this man disciplined him, reprimanded him at times, and taught him the laws of God and the universe. From him, Adam would have learned the law of cause and effect and the consequences of his actions. He was taught the knowledge of good and evil, but until now he was devoid of experience. Now that he was a man (more likely a teenager) he was pretty much on his own.

He had the responsibilities of being a gardener, in time he would have animals to befriend and take care of and, eventually, Adam would have a wife.

In this beautiful environment was the tree of life and, unlike his hominid cousins, Adam's superior brain could absorb all the wisdom this *tree* had to offer. However, beside the tree of life was the tree of the knowledge of good and evil, and as a human being he was responsible for his choices. If he chose to do evil he would die.

The *death* that the Bible speaks of in this passage has been misinterpreted many times over by scholars and preachers alike. I have even read of *experts* in theology who say that God later changed his mind and let Adam live after all.

In the Bible there is the physical death and there is the spiritual death. The physical death, as we know, is the death of the body, and it is permanent. When the body dies, it decays and returns to the dust from which it came. The soul will go on, but that particular body will NEVER, ever rise again. The spiritual death is a choice of evil behavior—wanting to be ignorant and refusing to eat the fruit of wisdom from the tree of life.

We were especially created to partake of the tree of life. Unlike the other creatures, we have the capacity for wisdom and understanding the *mysteries* of God. To choose not to partake of the tree of life is a will to be ignorant, foolish or evil and, in the biblical sense of the word, the soul is dead.

Unlike the death of the body, the spiritual death is not permanent. We can be spiritually alive whenever we make that decision; the choice is ours.

When evil is chosen, it transgresses the laws of God and nature. God is love and God is benevolent. Evil is the absence of love and is malevolent. Evil is death. "In the day that you eat thereof you shall surely die."

> *And the LORD God said, It is not good that the man should be alone; I will make an help mate for him.*
> *And out of the ground the LORD God formed every beast of the field, and every fowl of the air; and brought them to Adam to see what he would call them: and whatsoever Adam called every living creature, that was the name thereof.*
> *And Adam gave names to all cattle, and to the fowl of the air, and to every beast of the field; but for Adam there was not found an help mate for him.*
>
> Genesis 2:18 – 20

Adam now had his home in the garden and was caring for the trees and vegetation, but he was alone in this huge park. The LORD God said to the other members of his staff that it was not good for him to be alone. There was never a question that he would remain alone, of course, as he was to be the father of a modern people.

One will notice that it was out of the ground that the LORD God formed every beast of the field and fowl of the air; the same way that he formed Adam. Today we would say that he bred and crossbred some specially chosen livestock that would be suitable for the garden and compatible to the man and his future wife. Quite possibly, only the birds with colorful plumage and certain field animals were chosen. The LORD God brought them to Adam "to see what he would call them." Notice, too, that no water creatures or creeping crawling creatures were formed. That was because they were already there in rivers and on the ground—they didn't need an invitation.

The garden was now well populated and Adam got to know his animals by name. They would have been herbivores, and friendly ones at that because, after all, this was paradise.

Adam had a name and status as a human and he in turn gave status and names to his fellow creatures, each in its own right. He was Lord now, and had domain over the garden and the life that was in it.

It has always been thought that another author wrote these verses because they are contradictory to God creating everything in *six days*. There is no contradiction. God created everything in those six periods of time and set the forces of evolution in place. On the seventh day "he rested." There was no more creation after that, and most certainly not after the LORD God formed Adam. It was the LORD God who formed animals for the garden, just as we do with plants and animals today. There is no miracle and no contradiction, and I don't believe there were two authors.

ooo

Now we have Adam, a good looking, bright young man in a lush and gorgeous mirage, with only beasts and birds for companions. The original Tarzan of the jungle! Animals and birds offer a great deal of love and can make for great buddies, but despite being paradise, something was missing. Tarzan had a Jane. Adam did not.

"But for Adam there was not found an help mate for him."

These words say that the LORD God was *looking* for a mate for Adam, but could not *find* one that was suitable. He must have been searching for someone among the hominids that lived in the vicinity, and from which the genes of Adam were taken.

There is an old legend, one of many on the creation story, that tells of a woman named Lilith who was supposedly Adam's first wife. Where she came from or how she was chosen, the legend doesn't elaborate, but for reasons unknown the relationship did not go well. Whether she thought that Adam was too involved with his animals and away from home too much or that his gardening kept him so busy that he couldn't even take out the garbage, we'll never know. Perhaps she didn't like the LORD God and thought of him as an interfering old geezer. At any rate, she walked out on Adam and left the garden. I would assume that she went back home to her family, somewhere out there among the cave dwellers.

The legend goes on to say that Lilith became an evil spirit who crept around during the night and killed newborns—a curse put on her for leaving her man.

Women for generations after would wear an amulet while pregnant and then place it around the newborn infant's neck to keep Lilith away. Whenever there was a stillbirth or a baby found dead in the morning, it was the fault of Lilith.

In most legends there is a grain of truth, no matter how small. It was not that Lilith became an evil spirit, but rather that the LORD God brought in a woman from among the hominids and for whatever reason, it did not work out.

When the LORD God could not find a woman that was suitable to be the mother of a future race, he decided to make one that would be physically and intellectually equal to Adam.

> *And the LORD God caused a deep sleep to fall upon Adam, and he slept: and he took one of his ribs, and closed up the flesh instead thereof.*
>
> *And the rib, which the LORD God had taken from the man, made he a woman, and brought her unto the man*
>
> Genesis 2:21–22

> *And Adam said, This is now bone of my bones, and flesh of my flesh: she shall be called woman, because she was taken out of Man.*
> *Therefore shall a man leave his father and his mother, and shall cleave unto his wife: and they shall be one flesh.*
> *And they were both naked, the man and his wife, and were not ashamed.*
>
> Genesis 2:23–25

Adam was taken to the LORD God's operating room, anesthetized, and had a rib removed. It is highly unlikely that he was cut open under the apple tree, as I have seen in biblical story illustrations. Adam's rib was taken and used for its genetic material and whatever other *magic* the great doctor—the LORD God—needed to form a female embryo.

The scientists on our planet cannot currently clone a female from a male, but that does not mean it is impossible.

Adam was then stitched up, and would heal quickly in a peaceful setting of warmth, pure air, and plenty of fresh fruit.

The embryo would have then been planted into a surrogate mother and the birth would have gone naturally after that, as is the way of Mother Nature. The child would have been nurtured and cared for in the LORD God's home just as Adam was, and when she was old enough she was introduced to Adam in the garden. They would be most compatible because she was from his bone and his flesh. Although they may have been thirteen to twenty years apart in age, they were IDENTICAL TWINS.

The cloning of Adam and his wife/twin sister would ensure that this newly formed and perfect species of humankind would remain flawless and undefiled by stray and defective genes from other hominids out there in the wild.

The symbolism of this first union was enshrined for generations to come and was to be observed by husbands and wives within a marriage, and for men and women in general. They should cleave to each other as if they were of one flesh and bone. One was not dominant or to rule over the other, but side by side as if joined by a rib. Wow! Our world has really messed up in this area.

"And they were both naked...and were not ashamed."

Why should they be? They were young and attractive, of the same flesh, and they lived in an isolated, warm and sheltered garden among magnificent trees. However, it is not likely that the LORD God, his family or staff walked around naked, nor did Adam and Eve when they were children in his household. Why was this mentioned, and why was it significant to the story?

Adam and Eve were physically naked, meaning that they were not wearing any clothes, and they were not ashamed because they were as innocent as newborn babes were and as pure in heart. There is, however, a psychological form of nakedness that is mentioned in the Bible.

In Exodus 32:25, Moses came down from Mount Sinai and saw that his brother Aaron had taken the people's gold jewelry and made a golden calf for them to worship in his absence. Moses saw "that the people were naked" which meant that they had lost their pride and were without honor and substance. They were naked and ashamed before their enemies.

This psychological nakedness was eventually to creep into the garden of Eden.

8
Paradise Lost

Now the serpent was more subtil than any beast of the field which
the LORD God had made. And he said unto the woman,
Yea, has God said, You shall not eat of every tree in the garden?
And the woman said to the serpent, We may eat of the fruit of the
trees of the garden:
But of the fruit of the tree which is in the midst of the garden, God
has said, You shall not eat of it, neither shall you touch it, lest
you die.
And the serpent said to the woman, You shall not surely die:
For God does know that in the day you eat thereof, then your eyes
shall be opened, and you shall be as gods, knowing good and
evil.

Genesis 3:1 – 5

Serpents and Snakes, Reptiles and Dragons

THE serpent, or snake, is a member of the family of reptiles that has never endeared itself to any degree to humans, nor does it have many friends among other animals in the world. I have never heard of a snake being trained to fetch slippers and the newspaper or wag its tail in a friendly gesture. As far back as we can go in history and its mythology, the serpent has almost always been a symbol of fear, dread and evil.

The earliest reptiles were the various species of dinosaurs and from what we see of fossils, some of those big guys looked pretty fierce. They probably didn't have too many friends either. Among the dinosaurs were the biblical land animals called the behemoths and the water reptiles known as leviathans.

While the concept of evil was associated with the serpent or the dragon in many nations, some ancient cultures, such as those of Lemuria and Atlantis, apparently worshipped the serpent as having divine wisdom. There were stories of beings of great wisdom who descended from the skies to teach mankind on this planet, and they called themselves *Dragons* or *Serpent People*. It was said that China chose the emblem of the dragon in their honor, and believed the Celestial Dragon to be the Father of the First Dynasty.

When Jesus gathered around him those who would be his disciples, he told them that they would be sent out to teach as sheep among the wolves, and that they would have to be as "wise as serpents, and harmless as doves." (Matthew 10:16)

The snake is a cunning and crafty creature and wise in its own way. It waits unseen and without motion for its unsuspecting prey. It knows exactly who it wants and what it wants. Then swiftly and silently, it strikes the unaware—there is no escape, only death. Thus is evil personified as a serpent.

> *"Now the serpent was more subtil than any beast of the field which the LORD God had made."*

The animals in the garden that the LORD God had bred especially for companionship for the young couple were domesticated, unlike those in the wild. They were tame and friendly and able to communicate in their own way, just as we do with our pets today. But the serpent was more subtle than they were. Why would there be a serpent in the garden of paradise?

The serpent was not an earthly creature. It was NOT one of the animals in the garden. IT WAS EVIL PERSONIFIED. It was evil thoughts in the mind of Eve, and evil thoughts are *more subtle* than any animal on earth.

> *"And he said unto the woman...has God said, You shall not eat of every tree of the garden?"*

Here we have *God* entering into the questioning. Until now it was only the LORD God who taught these two people everything that they had to know to be human. He taught them about God and the knowledge of good and evil, but Eve (in her mind) is now questioning the teachings of the LORD God. They were told that they could eat from every tree that was in the garden, but they were not to touch temptation. They were to stay within the laws of God the Creator if they wanted to live the way that God had intended for his creation. If they did otherwise, they would die the spiritual death and experience separation from the Spirit.

The LORD God must be wrong, she thought. Why would God punish us with spiritual death if he gave humans the knowledge (above all animals) of good and evil? If we know what is good and what is evil and we have been given a choice, then what is so bad about trying out some of the actions referred to as evil? Should we not then be as gods—to really know good and evil?

Of course we are gods simply because we have that knowledge, but what Eve did not think of was that we are also responsible for our actions, our behavior and even for our thoughts, and although the spirit is willing, it is the flesh that is weak. And that is why Adam and Eve were admonished (as we still are) not to eat of the fruit of evil, "lest we die."

> *"And the serpent said to the woman, You shall not surely die…For God does know…your eyes shall be opened, and you shall be as gods. …"*

Now in this era we would call the serpent *the devil*, or *Satan*. When we are tempted to do something that we know is wrong, we say "the devil made me do it." Eve was tempted. The LORD God had said that the tree of the knowledge of good and evil would always be in their midst; wherever they were in the world and in their lives they would always have to choose the right or the wrong way. Why then were they kept there in the garden, closed in and away from the rest of the world—like children? Why were they not allowed to grow up, experience life and be gods like the LORD God and his people? God had made them to have dominion on the earth and to be gods, she was sure of that. The LORD God was wrong, and too restrictive.

A parallel to Eve's thinking would be the teenagers of today who can't wait to grow up. They want to leave the confines of home, sneak into bars, stretch curfews and light that first cigarette, but they do not realize the consequences of their actions and the responsibilities of being an adult.

> *And when the woman saw that the tree was good for food, and that it was pleasant to the eyes, and a tree to be desired to make one wise, she took of the fruit thereof, and did eat, and gave also unto her husband with her; and he did eat.*
> *And the eyes of them both were opened, and they knew that they were naked; and they sewed fig leaves together, and made themselves aprons.*
>
> Genesis 3:6–7

The Fruit

The garden of Eden was not to be Adam and Eve's permanent home. Eventually, as they grew more knowledgeable in the ways of God and nature, they would go forth and replenish the planet. The young woman, in the course of time, however, may have become restless and turned her thoughts to that mysterious world out there beyond the garden gate. Ready or not, she might have wanted to grow up and leave home. The tree of the knowledge of good and evil looked pleasant to the eyes and enticing to think about. Its many choices of fruit could only make one wise, and one would need experience in order to gain wisdom. Right? So she ate of the fruit, and gave some to her husband and he also ate.

It is not recorded what that *fruit* was, and no it was not an apple. It was a sin, a transgression that would disrupt the teaching and learning process that was the original purpose of the garden. The first *sons of God* were to learn how to live the kingdom of God and heaven and partake of the *rest* that was ordained in the beginning. They were to learn and then teach their children and their children's children after them, and make this world into a paradise on earth.

In the book of Jeremiah (14:10), the prophet says: "Thus says the LORD to this people, They have loved to wander, they have not refrained their feet. …"

Did Adam and Eve perhaps wander away from the garden on occasion? Maybe after the LORD God had retired for the day and gone back to Eden to his lounging chair and glass of wine, they would sneak out and have a look around.

"And the eyes of them both were opened. ..."

What they would have seen were people wild and free doing whatever they wanted to do, people living a life that Adam and Eve were not allowed to live, and they had no LORD God constantly on their backs. What they also would have noticed was that the people wore the skins of animals, unlike the gods in Eden. They realized that they were naked, innocent and childlike compared to those out there in the world, and they wanted to be like them. They wanted to be worldly. "...and they sewed fig leaves together, and made themselves aprons."

And they heard the voice of the LORD God walking in the cool of the day: and Adam and his wife hid themselves from the presence of the LORD God amongst the trees of the garden.

And the LORD God called unto Adam, and said unto him, Where are you?

And he said, I heard your voice in the garden, and I was afraid, because I was naked; and I hid myself.

And he said, Who told you that you were naked? Have you eaten of the tree, whereof I commanded you that you should not eat?

And the man said, The woman whom you gave to be with me, she gave me of the tree, and I did eat.

And the LORD God said unto the woman, What is this that you have done? And the woman said, The serpent beguiled me, and I did eat.

And the LORD God said unto the serpent, Because you have done this, you are cursed above all cattle, and above every beast of the field; upon your belly shall you go, and dust shall you eat all the days of your life.

Genesis 3:8 – 14

> *And I will put enmity between you and the woman, and between your seed and her seed; it shall bruise your head, and you shall bruise his heel.*
>
> Genesis 3:15

They Made a Choice

> *"And they heard the voice of the LORD God walking in the cool of the day. . . ."*

These words are proof that this was not God the Almighty or even the LORD God of heaven. It is only an earthly man that walks down a garden path in the cool of the day and talks in a voice that can be heard by two people hiding amongst the trees.

It was not that Adam and Eve were ashamed of their nakedness and had covered themselves with fig leaves that concerned the LORD God, but that they had disobeyed him and demonstrated to him that they were losing interest in a spiritual life in favor of a more physical existence.

In time, when he knew that they were ready, he would have slowly introduced them to the world outside. After they had grown enough in awareness of the consequences of their actions and their choices in life, he would have prepared them to leave home. He would have probably dressed them in colorful silks and linens, rather than animal skins, and taught them to live in the spirit while still in the flesh.

His mission on this planet was to develop a genetic blueprint for a new, more modern hominid, and to bring the species up to the level of other advanced nations in the cosmos. It disappointed and angered him that he would be unable to complete his work to his satisfaction because of their disobedience.

Although Adam was formed from a specially selected genetic pool and Eve was his clone, they still carried within them their evolutionary past. They, like all the other life on the planet, were from the dust of the earth and what the "ground had brought forth." They were still the *sons of men.*

Had they stayed faithful to the teachings of the LORD God, it would only have been a matter of time until someone would have "sinned." If Cain and Abel had been born in the garden of Eden, chances are there would have been a murder in paradise. Cain would have snapped a branch from one of those magnificent trees and clubbed Abel into the ground.

Given the combination of superior brain power and the knowledge of good and evil, it is inevitable that some of these higher life forms will choose evil and continue to choose evil until the end of time, as we know it.

> Wherefore, as by one man sin entered into the world, and death by sin; and so death passed upon all men, for that all have sinned: For until the law sin was in the world: but sin is not imputed when there is no law. Nevertheless death reigned from Adam to Moses, even over them that had not sinned after the similitude of Adam's transgression, who is the figure of him that was to come.
>
> Romans 5:12–14

What this means is that the first law for mankind was put on this planet when Adam, the first Homo sapien, came into being. Unlike all the other species of hominids that were present at that time, Adam knew right from wrong, had the knowledge of good and evil, and was able to choose how he wanted to live. Before Adam and Eve, there was good and evil because they are the dimensions of God and nature, but they were not sins. Sin is a transgression of the law, and any action or behavior was not labeled (imputed) as good or evil.

Although the Bible does not say exactly what sin the first couple committed, there is only one sin that will result in spiritual death and that is the transgression of the law of communion with God: the cosmic union of body and soul. Adam and Eve were made special to be *sons of God*, but when they wandered away from their spiritual lessons, they chose evil over good and that meant they preferred living completely in the physical.

> *"And the man said, The woman whom you gave to be with me, she gave me of the tree, and I did eat."*

Out pours the thoughts of a typical human being, son of God or not—blame someone else...anyone!

In the Talmud, Rabbi Yose Ben Johanan of Jerusalem instructed his students to study the Torah every day, and to discuss it with men as much as possible, but "talk not so much with women, even with one's own wife...So long as a man talks overmuch with women, he brings evil upon himself. . . ."[1]

No comment.

> *"And the LORD God said unto the woman, What is this that you have done? And the woman said, The serpent beguiled me, and I did eat."*

The devil made me do it!

> *"And the LORD God said unto the serpent. . .you are cursed above all cattle, and above every beast of the field; upon your belly shall you go, and dust shall you eat all the days of your life."*

Animals are destined to live within the confines of their evolutionary paths. They cannot grow in wisdom or grasp the reasoning between good and evil. They cannot sin, and their innocent lives depend solely on nature and on the whims of the people who have dominion over them. In that sense, they are inferior to humans, and in the biblical sense, they are cursed.

The snake as evil personified was cursed *above* all cattle and *above* every beast of the field. The serpent of evil was inferior to any living thing on earth.

The ninety-seven million year old fossilized remains of a serpent with very small hind legs that was found in Israel could well have been the ancestor of the slithering snake of today. The fossil no longer had forearms. Maybe during the time of Adam and Eve (As stated, approximately 200,000 years ago), some of the reptiles began to appear without limbs of any kind, and it was attributed to a curse from God. Or just maybe the LORD God intentionally manipulated the genetic code of some local snakes to prove his point, and to illustrate what a curse really is.

The image that King Nebuchadnezzer placed on the gates of Babylon was a *footed serpent*, and the Sumerian poem spoke of a time *before* there were snakes and scorpions.

> *"And dust shall you eat. . . ."*

Snakes do not eat dust, they eat small animals and birds, and the larger the snake, the larger its prey. It is amazing what a snake can do without limbs. The Bible, however, is not talking about the earthly snake. It is referring to the serpent that is the symbol of evil, and this serpent eats *dust*. *WE ARE DUST*. We are made of the dust of the earth, as is all matter, and when we remove ourselves from the spiritual life that was our heritage and eat of the fruit of evil, as did Adam and Eve, we will be prey for him that eats dust. That is the SPIRITUAL DEATH.

> *"And I will put enmity between you and the woman, and between your seed and her seed. ..."*

The seed of the woman are the sons of God, who in the beginning were the Adamic race of mankind. Later the sons of God were, and still are, all who accept the spiritual way of life and the union of body and soul. From the seed of woman also came the Son of God and the Son of man (Jesus). The seed of the serpent of evil are the *sons of men*—those who choose evil over good and do not acknowledge the spirit within them.

> *"...it shall bruise your head, and you shall bruise his heel."*

The woman's seed cannot destroy evil because evil is a dimension of God and it can only bruise its head. Evil could not and cannot completely destroy the seed of woman, and when the Son of man was nailed to the cross two thousand years ago by the seed of the serpent of evil, it only managed to bruise *his* heel.

> He that sows the good seed is the Son of man: The field is the world; the good seed are the children of the kingdom; but the tares are the children of the wicked one; The enemy that sowed them is the devil. ... Matthew 13:37–39

> And the great dragon was cast out, that old serpent, called the Devil, and Satan, which deceived the whole world. ... Revelation 12:9

Unto the woman he said, I will greatly multiply your sorrow and your conception; in sorrow you shall bring forth children; and your desire shall be to your husband, and he shall rule over you.
And unto Adam he said, Because you have hearkened unto the voice of your wife, and have eaten of the tree, of which I commanded you, saying, You shall not eat of it: cursed is the ground for your sake, in sorrow shall you eat of it all the days of your life;
Thorns and thistles shall it bring forth to you; and you shall eat of the herb of the field;
In the sweat of your face shall you eat bread, till you return to the ground; for out of it you were taken: for dust you are, and unto dust shall you return.

Genesis 3:16 – 19

The guilt complex was already well developed in Adam and Eve when they realized how naked they were and draped themselves in fig leaves. Only humans know guilt. Animals can share the same emotions that we have; they know happiness and sorrow, anger and fear, and they experience love and hate, but they do not have guilt, nor do they need to. Guilt is strictly a human condition and results when an action is taken that one knows is wrong, and only humans can do wrong.

Eve knew that she had disobeyed the LORD God and all that he had to do to punish her was to suggest to her that she would bear her future children in pain and sorrow. He was not only angry, he knew his psychology very well. The young couple had not learned all there was to learn in the garden before they began to stray from their teachings, and they had not yet taken Psychology 101 and the power of suggestion.

The LORD God told Eve that he will greatly multiply her pain and sorrow. If he could make her and Adam then she probably thought that he could do that, too. He was, after all, a god from the sky. He also said that she would be subservient to her husband and that he would rule over her. That would sound reasonable to her now that her self-esteem was crushed. She did lead the poor man astray, did she not? She would have to pay for her transgression in childbirth, and be a servant to her husband—she and her daughters down through the generations.

Apparently, it did not dawn on Eve that she was of the same flesh and bone as her husband and from his side, not from his foot to be kicked around. She was his clone and equal in status and intelligence "for therefore shall a man leave his father and his mother, and shall cleave to his wife; and they shall be *one flesh*."

To Adam also the LORD God handed out some pretty strong suggestions. He *did not* curse the ground as some people think. What he said was, "cursed *is* the ground *for your sake....*" It was Adam who would inadvertently curse the ground with his own thoughts, attitudes and beliefs. *He* would make his life tough and hard to bear, and he would *think* that he must work and sweat and grow weary. And he would pass on the legacy to his sons and their sons after them.

Adam and Eve had caused their own fate, and that was what the LORD God was demonstrating to them. They had tasted the fruit of evil by questioning the laws that the LORD God had been sent to teach them, and they cut short their stay in the garden before their lessons were complete. What they would have learned was the cosmic union of body and soul, the *rest* that God ordained for all of his children, the power of THOUGHT, and the mysteries of the kingdom of God and heaven. They would have learned that heaven and hell is *within* us, and we alone choose which one to live.

> *And Adam called his wife's name Eve; because she was the mother of all living.*
> *Unto Adam also and to his wife did the LORD God make coats of skins, and clothed them.*
> *And the LORD God said, the man is become as one of us, to know good and evil: and now, lest he put forth his hand, and take also of the tree of life, and eat, and live forever:*
> *Therefore the LORD God sent him forth from the garden of Eden, to till the ground from whence he was taken.*
>
> Genesis 3:20–23

> *So he drove out the man; and he placed at the east of the garden of Eden Cherubims, and a flaming sword which turned every way, to keep the way of the tree of life.*
>
> Genesis 3:24

The Wages of Sin

Adam knew that there was quite a different lifestyle waiting for them out there in the world and they needed to be prepared for it. The LORD God knew what had to be done and the first thing he did was to dress them in animal skins so they would be like their new neighbors. No doubt he would have taught them housekeeping in a cave, how to grow food, and how to hunt down animals for the kill. It was now a cold, cruel world and no longer paradise. Adam knew, however, that they were still destined to be the parents of a novel race of the sons of men, and he called his wife *Eve* because, eventually, she would be the mother of all living.

> *"And the LORD God said, the man is become as one of us...."*

The various species of hominids in the region and in the world were not at the level of development as were the visitors from the sky, but Adam and Eve were. They had the knowledge of good and evil—the one distinction between human and animal. The LORD God was angry, frustrated and disappointed in the failure of his project, and he knew that intelligence without the spiritual knowledge of God could make for a dangerous people. They could become the seeds of the serpent of evil.

He did not want Adam and his wife to take of the tree of life and live forever. The tree of life in the garden was the metaphor of the wisdom and the mysteries of God that we all need to know to attain the kingdom of heaven/God that is within us. Adam and Eve left the garden before they learned this most important lesson.

The tree of life is also the source of all living things: "the Spirit that moved upon the face of the waters." The LORD God did not want this wayward couple to partake of the physical tree of life that is the breath of all that has life. Perhaps it would be best if, now that they were amongst the hominids, they would interbreed themselves into oblivion. He did not think that the species he had formed should live forever down through the ages. In evolution, some die and become extinct, and maybe they should also die.

> "*...he placed at the east of the garden of Eden Cherubims, and a flaming sword which turned every way, to keep the way of the tree of life.*"

After the couple and the animals were removed from the garden, the entrance on the east side was closed off. That would be what is now the Gulf of Oman.

In the course of time, and due perhaps to an earthquake or the melting of an early ice age, the sea rose and encroached into the rivers that flowed through the garden, and these rivers became what is now the Persian Gulf. Maybe the LORD God knew that this would eventually take place so he put what might have been an electronic device or a pillar with pulsating lights at the entrance together with the Cherubims. Why the east entrance and not the west, which would have been facing Eden? This is a mystery to me. Nor does it say how many Cherubims, what their purpose was or what kind they were.

In this verse the word *Cherubim* is capitalized and, as I mentioned in Chapter Two, the King James Bible initially capitalizes words that have a double meaning. Since no more is mentioned in Genesis about the LORD God being present, these Cherubim may have been the aircraft that came to take him and his team home.

In biblical times, the people (the general public) did not understand the various forces of energy or light, and they would describe it as fire that does not consume, or "the glory of God."

> "*A flaming sword which turned every way, to keep the way of the tree of life.*"

In the Bible, the sword is a symbol of war and an instrument of death. The flame is an energy that consumes everything in its path. The mind is the most powerful force of energy in heaven and earth because it is spirit from the Spirit—a part of God the Energy and the Light. The power of thought can create for the good that is the God in us, or it can be an all-consuming flame of evil that destroys everything in its path.

Our first parents made their choice, and we make ours still on the same planet thousands of years later. The flaming sword of war, rumors of war and death have been with us from the beginning of our status as humans, and it is still of our choosing today. It is our *THOUGHT* that turns every way to keep us from the *tree of life*, and with the flaming sword is paradise lost.

NOTES

[1] Goldin, J. (1957). *The Living Talmud*. New York, NY: The New American Library, p. 54.

9
Giants and Men of Renown

And Adam knew Eve his wife; and she conceived, and bare Cain, and said, I have gotten a man from the LORD.
And she again bare his brother Abel. And Abel was a keeper of sheep, but Cain was a tiller of the ground.
And in the process of time it came to pass, that Cain brought of the fruit of the ground an offering unto the LORD.
And Abel, he also brought of the firstlings of his flock and of the fat thereof. And the LORD had respect unto Abel and to his offering.
But unto Cain and to his offering he had not respect. And Cain was very wroth, and his countenance fell.
And the LORD said unto Cain, Why are you wroth? and why is your countenance fallen?
If you do well, shall you not be accepted? and if you do not well, sin lies at the door. And to you shall be his desire, and you shall rule over him.

Genesis 4:1–7

Cain and Abel

ADAM and Eve now lived west of the garden in the land of Eden, that was much later known as *Mesopotamia: the Cradle of Civilization*. The LORD God had dressed them in skins and prepared them for the caveman life. He would have taught Adam how to make tools to cultivate the ground, or maybe he gave him his first tools. Their fruit-plucking days were over.

A very ancient Sumerian legend (7000 BC) tells of how *Enlil*, the god who had separated the waters of heaven and earth, came down and gave the first people tools with which to build, and taught them agriculture. A subconscious memory handed down from the misty past?[1]

> *"And Eve bore a son and named him Cain, and said, I have gotten a man from the LORD."*

She did not say the *LORD God* because he was no longer there.

After the LORD God got them settled in Eden amongst the other people, he and his team packed up, and left the planet.

Adam and Eve had learned enough about God the Creator while in the garden, and they were told of the LORD who would care for them through the process of thought, meditation and prayer. His name was *Jehovah*, and he was a spirit. Adam and Eve would no longer have an earthly contact.

The LORD God was dissatisfied with the man and woman he had formed and he felt that it might be best if they became extinct (not live forever), but Adam and Eve did survive. They were still the *sons of God*, in contrast to their neighbors who were the *sons of men*. They were different from the people around them; they were more intelligent, more refined in appearance, and they knew right from wrong. From Adam and Eve would come giants and men of renown.

When Cain was born, Eve knew for certain that she and Adam had the blessing of the LORD from heaven. They would be the parents of a new people after all, and Eve would be the mother of all living! And she bore another son, and named him *Abel*.

The Bible literally tells us that Cain was a farmer and Abel was a shepherd. So what is wrong with that? Each of these boys had chosen the lifestyle that interested him and they were doing what they most enjoyed. Their dad had started out as a gardener, and was now a caveman of all trades. They all had legitimate occupations. Why then was the LORD displeased with Cain's offering? For the answer we have to read these verses very carefully.

This is not just a story of two young brothers, but there is in it a powerful message for all humankind.

Cain "brought of the fruit of the ground an offering unto the LORD." That was it—just an offering: as little as he could get away with and still be thought of as a nice guy. Now Abel also gave an offering—"the firstlings of his flock and of the fat thereof." He gave the best that he had, even the fat—a precious commodity in ancient times.

Cain's thankfulness was half-hearted and on the surface. He offered nothing of himself, but rather gave only what the ground (the physical/worldly) had to offer. Abel, on the other hand, was caring and conscientious and when he offered the best that he had, it was like giving of himself. Perfection in thought and deed was Abel's calling, and the LORD respected that. This left Cain discouraged and angry.

Cain had a bad attitude. He expected and craved respect, but did not feel that he needed to reciprocate. Anger, discouragement and depression were the traits of his personality that he had chosen for himself and that no one had inflicted on him. They were totally of his own making, but that was not the way he saw it. He blamed his brother for making him look bad.

Through his conscience, or perhaps in a dream, the LORD spoke with Cain and reminded him that if he did not change his attitude, sin—like a serpent—would lie at the door waiting to be let in. Cain knew (from his parents) that he could overrule his sinful thoughts if he so desired; he had a choice between good and evil.

> *And Cain talked with Abel his brother: and it came to pass, when they were in the field, that Cain rose up against Abel his brother, and slew him.*
>
> *And the LORD said unto Cain, Where is Abel your brother? And he said, I know not: Am I my brother's keeper?*
>
> *And he said, What have you done? The voice of your brother's blood cries unto me from the ground.*
>
> *And now you are cursed from the earth, which has opened her mouth to receive your brother's blood from your hand.*
>
> Genesis 4:8 – 11

When you till the ground, it shall not henceforth yield unto you her strength; a fugitive and a vagabond shall you be in the earth.
And Cain said unto the LORD. My punishment is greater than I can bear.
Behold you have driven me out this day from the face of the earth; and from your face shall I be hidden, and I shall be a fugitive and a vagabond in the earth; and it shall come to pass, that every one that finds me shall slay me.
And the LORD said unto him, Therefore whosoever slays Cain, vengeance shall be taken on him sevenfold. And the LORD set a mark upon Cain, lest any finding him should kill him.

Genesis 4:12–15

Cain killed his brother, and he knew what he did was wrong and a sin. He could hear his LORD'S words in his mind, "Where is Abel your brother?" Defiantly, he answered his own question, "Am I my brother's keeper?" Then the guilt and remorse overtook him and he knew that he would have to answer to the LORD in heaven.

"The voice of your brother's blood cries unto me from the ground."

Cain was certain that he heard the LORD'S voice, and he knew that he had been cursed from the earth that opened its mouth to receive Abel's blood.

He could still hear his brother's cries as his blood soaked into the ground, and he would hear them forever after. How could he possibly continue to till the soil and tend to a crop that was drenched with the blood of his brother?

His strength was gone, and so was his will to farm the land. The LORD and the earth cursed him, and he would be a vagabond and a fugitive for the rest of his life.

And then there were his parents…they had taught him right from wrong, and now he had dashed the hopes and dreams of the future they imagined for both of their sons. He could no longer live with them and watch their anguish. He would have to leave home.

Cain wrestled with his thoughts and his guilt, and prayed to the LORD like he had never prayed before, but he did not ask for forgiveness. His sin was too great for that, and it was even greater than he could bear. He was a son of God whose heritage would now be taken away from him, and he would have to leave Eden and live among the sons of men in a distant land. It would be survival of the fittest out in the wilderness, and Cain feared that he would be killed. He was different from the people that he would be in contact with, and even today we know what a slight difference can cause among people—civilized or not.

> *"And the LORD set a mark upon Cain, lest any finding him should kill him."*

What the mark was is not mentioned in the Bible, but one Jewish writing states that Cain was stricken with palsy as a punishment for his crime. That is highly unlikely. An illness of any kind would have made him more vulnerable to attack from a primitive people, and in that condition he could not have made the trek to a distant land.

The mark that Cain received was more of a benefit to him than a hindrance. After all, he was the son of Adam and Eve; he was likely taller and had a more modern physique, and was smarter with a charismatic personality. In our society he could be described as having sex appeal. His mark was something that would draw people to him. Maybe when they first saw him they thought he was a god who had come to help them live a better life—like the ones they had seen on various occasions. And help them he did. This god did not come from the sky, and he did not go back up into the sky and disappear. He stayed...and built a city.

> *And Cain went out from the presence of the LORD, and dwelt in the land of Nod, on the east of Eden.*
> *And Cain knew his wife; and she conceived, and bare Enoch: and he builded a city, and called the name of the city, after the name of his son, Enoch.*
>
> Genesis 4:16–17

And unto Enoch was born Irad...begat Mehujael...begat Lamech.
And Lamech took unto him two wives...Adah...Zillah.
And Zillah bare Jabal...the father of such as dwell in tents, and of such as have cattle.
And his brother's name was Jubal: he was the father of all such as handle the harp and organ.
And Zillah, she also bare Tubal-Cain, an instructor of every artificer in brass and iron: and the sister of Tubal-Cain was Naamah.
And Lamech said unto his wives...I have slain a man to wounding, and a young man to my hurt.
If Cain shall be avenged sevenfold, truly Lamech seventy and sevenfold.
And Adam knew his wife again; and she bare a son, and called his name Seth: For God, said she, has appointed me another seed instead of Abel, whom Cain slew.
And to Seth, to him also there was born a son; and he called his name Enos: then began men to call upon the name of the LORD.

Genesis 4:18–26

Throughout the Bible, from the patriarchs to the apostles, the writers have all used Cain as the symbol of evil, in contrast to Abel, the good. They have made him appear unredeemable. That is not what the Bible says. No, his seed would no longer be with the sons of God, but he was still of the superior species of mankind and carried the mark of the knowledge of good and evil.

He chose a wife from the land of Nod, which was east of Eden and what today would be eastern Saudi Arabia, or Iran. Directly east of Eden, of course, was the garden of Eden and what is now the Persian Gulf. Maybe in Cain's time there was no Gulf yet, and that *was* where Nod was located.

Cain was remorseful for his crime and resolved to change his life for the better. He built a city and became the leader and the patriarch of his own race of people. He now had a positive attitude and good morals, and he taught them to his children and their children after them. They knew what was good and what was evil, and had heard from Cain what his crime had been.

He was no longer under the guidance of the LORD Jehovah, but he was still a son of God—physically, intellectually and spiritually. His hybrid children inherited his qualities and became inventors, discoverers and artisans.

The final verses in the epic of Cain give us insight into a time and place where some hominid groups had reached the level of almost modern. They were intelligent enough to build a society and live in tents instead of caves. The genetics of Cain into this group could only be an enhancement.

While Cain was starting a new life some distance away, his mother had another son whom she named Seth. He was sent to them from God, they were certain of that, and through him would emerge the unadulterated lineage of the sons of God. Down through the generations, the sons of God would learn about *God* the Creator and call on the name of the *LORD* for guidance.

This is the book of the generations of Adam. In the day that God created man, in the likeness of God made he him;
Male and female created he them, and blessed them, and called their name Adam, in the day when they were created.
And Adam lived a hundred and thirty years, and begat a son in his own likeness, after his image; and called his name Seth.
And the days of Adam after he had begotten Seth were eight hundred years; and he begat sons and daughters:
And all the days that Adam lived were nine hundred and thirty years: and he died.

Genesis 5:1–5

This is the book of the first generations of the Homo sapiens, male and female, created in God's image and likeness, and he called their name *Adam*.

From Genesis 5:6 to Genesis 5:29, the chronology from Adam to Noah includes ten patriarchs of their respective generations. From Adam to the birth of Noah was 1056 years in our time calculations. Assuming that all the names and ages from Adam to Noah are correct—who kept a record? And who wrote them down?

The extremely lengthy lifespan of these people does not make sense to us today. Perhaps the years were measured differently, or maybe these ancient souls knew some mysteries of life that have long been forgotten.

Then, too, we have only the names of the key characters in this biblical saga. The names that are mentioned were the fathers, patriarchs and leaders of their extended families, and they were endowed with extraordinary wisdom and talents. They were spiritual and psychic, and it was through them that the LORD Jehovah communicated to the sons of God. This whole race of people may have been stronger and healthier and lived longer than the general population of hominids; but maybe it was only the patriarchs that lived that long.

If the story of Adam and the chronology of the other nine patriarchs are myths, it is not likely that there would be exact ages, births and deaths and even names of each of the fathers of their generations. Myths and legends do not usually go into such detail. It appears that a well-preserved journal was kept and handed down by very responsible persons who were giants amongst their people—and men of renown.

Genesis Chapter Five mentions the book of the generations of the Adamic race. The Jewish *Zohar* tells of a book known as *The Secret Doctrine*, or *The Supreme Book*, that was brought down from heaven and given to Adam by the angel Raziel. When Adam left the garden the book was taken away from him, but with his pleas, tears and prayers, the angel Raphael brought it back to him.

Adam later bequeathed the book to his son Seth, and on to each of the patriarchs. When it got to Enoch it had deteriorated, so he rewrote it and it was then called *The Book of Enoch*. It was said that Moses was the first to attain perfection in its fullness, and after Abraham nothing more was heard of the secret text. It vanished forever.

It is not too difficult to believe that Adam and Eve would have known how to read and write. During their childhood the LORD God, who came from a very spiritually and scientifically advanced planet, would have tutored them. And the Jewish legend is not that far-fetched either when it stated that the angel Raziel brought the book to Adam to study and add his own life story to it. The angel from heaven, no doubt, would have been from the heavens rather than heaven, and Raziel could well have been the name of the LORD God. It is only logical to think that Adam and Eve learned and spoke the language of the LORD God and his people, and the book would have also been in their language.

Another legend has it that the original Hebrew alphabet came from heaven and that the Torah was written in heaven and brought down to this planet. In it were the laws of God for mankind and the secrets and mysteries of God and nature.

Whatever the "book" was, it was physical and made of matter. How it was made and what it looked like is unknown, but from it the Torah was born and my imagination tells me that knowledge in book form has been passed from planet to planet among the many waters. When it was our turn, when the sons of men became the sons of God, they were taught to read and write the knowledge of good and evil. Adam, our first human (Homo sapien) father, would add his autobiography, as would the others. From them the Bible evolved and, along with us, continues to evolve.

Archeologists have always wondered and marveled at how civilizations would spring up out of nowhere from very primitive people, and sometimes alongside primitive races.

We are not alone! We have neighbors! Neighbors tend to help each other on occasion.

And it came to pass, when men began to multiply on the face of the earth, and daughters were born unto them,
That the sons of God saw the daughters of men that they were fair; and they took them wives of all which they chose.
And the LORD said, My spirit shall not always strive with man, for that he also is flesh: yet his days shall be a hundred and twenty years.
There were giants in the earth in those days; and also after that, when the sons of God came in unto the daughters of men, and they bare children to them, the same became mighty men which were of old, men of renown.

Genesis 6:1–4

The Sons of God—Men of Renown

There is no record of how many sons and daughters Adam and Eve had; only Seth is mentioned after Cain since he was the patriarch of his generation. In order for this new and superior species to remain unadulterated, Seth would have had to marry a sister. Unlike Cain, who left his people and took a wife from another species of humans, Seth and most of his siblings would have married only each other to keep their bloodline intact. They were not to assimilate with the sons of men—out there in the wild.

These brothers and sisters were born of two people who were also brother and sister, and identical twins at that. There would have been nothing dysfunctional in their genes; they were free of disease or illness and this inbreeding would have meant strength rather than a weakness.

In a short time there would be aunts, uncles, nieces, nephews and cousins galore. Seth married his sister and his son would have married his cousin, and soon after there would be numerous choices.

The extended family kept to itself and grew into a city, and then a small nation. They were the sons of God, gifted with high intelligence and an up-to-date physique. They were the beautiful people of the world, but only in a very small section of the planet.

In the rest of the world various species of hominids were multiplying "on the face of the earth." In the Bible, these were the sons of men—from whom the sons of God originated.

In the area where the sons of God lived, a certain group of sons of men had almost reached the same level of physical attributes as the sons of God (the first Homo sapiens) and their daughters "were fair and they took them wives of all which they chose." Because of this, the genetic components of the sons of God became contaminated with genes that were meant to die out during the evolutionary process, as would all of the hominid species except the Homo sapiens.

With his servant, the LORD God, the LORD of heaven established a new species, and when he saw that his project was failing, he said, "My spirit shall not always strive with man, for that he also is flesh." In other words, he was tired of trying to keep this group of humans free from contamination. They were, after all, only flesh, and flesh can never be perfect. All of nature has its time to be born and its time to die, and man shall be the same. His days shall be within the range of a hundred and twenty years, and not much more than that.

When the sons of God married the daughters of men, their children became the *giants* of old and *men of renown*. It began when Cain married a woman from the land of Nod and his descendants were inventors, discoverers and artists. The word *giant* may have meant that they had giant intellect, but it could also refer to these people as being taller and stronger than were their parents and grandparents.

Homer, at the *Siege of Troy* wrote about the wise King Nestor who lived in an earlier time when men lived who were the strongest men that "Earth has bred…men whom not a soul on earth today could face in a battle."[2]

Whether some of these men were of giant stature is a matter of speculation. There is, however, the story of Goliath, whom David slew with a rock to his brain (1 Samuel 17), but he was an oddity among the Philistines who were of normal stature.

There are many biblical stories that portray the sons of God as angels that came down to marry women. Angels are spirits. They do not have physical bodies, and they do not reproduce like the creatures of the earth. They were created from the Light that is God and they are higher in status than humankind of the earth. Nor were the sons of God from another planet. The travelers and curiosity seekers from other planets who visited parts of our world in early times were thought of as gods and goddesses because they came from the sky, but they were not the sons of God.

An interesting myth from India states that, in ancient times, "seductive nymphs from the waters of space" came down and seduced the men of this earth.

From the sons of God and the daughters of men came the giants and men of renown who had acquired a very high level of intelligence and knowledge, but lost to them was the wisdom of the Spirit of God and the spirit within them. They were giants in mind, but not in soul.

NOTES

[1] Cottrell, L. (1962). *The Horizon Book of Lost Worlds*. New York, NY: American Heritage Publishing Co., p. 122.

[2] Cottrell, L. (1962). *The Horizon Book of Lost Worlds*. New York, NY: American Heritage Publishing Co., p. 20.

10
Shem, Ham, and Japheth

> *And God saw that the wickedness of man was great in the earth, and that every imagination of the thoughts of his heart was only evil continually.*
> *And it repented the LORD that he had made man on the earth, and it had grieved him at his heart.*
> *And the LORD said, I will destroy man whom I have created from the face of the earth; both man, and beast, and the creeping thing, and the fowls of the air; for it repents me that I have made them.*
> *But Noah found grace in the eyes of the LORD.*
> *These are the generations of Noah: Noah was a just man and perfect in his generations, and Noah walked with God.*
>
> Genesis 6:5–9

Noah

GOD is CONSCIOUS Energy and Light, and is aware at all times of what goes on in his creation. On this planet, the specially made species of humankind called the sons of God had hybridized themselves with a genetically inferior hominid group and forgotten the spirit within them. Their wickedness was great and their thoughts were evil continually.

The LORD of heaven was grieved that they had turned out bereft of the knowledge of God, and he was sorry that he had made them. Just as the LORD God had wanted to eliminate them through the process of assimilation in the beginning, so the LORD Jehovah felt that his spirit could not always strive with this wayward species.

The sons of God were now once again referred to as *man*, just as they once were in their primate state on the sixth day of creation. Man was highly intelligent and had the knowledge of good and evil, but lacked the morals of the spirit. There was no limit to what he could accomplish—or destroy.

The sons of God were to be good stewards over the rest of creation: to care for the flora and the fauna like they would a beautiful garden—"to dress it and to keep it." They were at the top of the evolutionary ladder and, unlike all that were below them, they could communicate with God and know the spirit within.

Because of their wickedness and the evil imaginations of their thoughts, however, their days as the sons of God were numbered; they would have to be destroyed.

Down through their first generations, they chose the physical over the spiritual (mammon over God), and their cleverness in the fields of science and technology might have reached the level where the environment was in danger. They were the giants and men of renown on this planet, and they were capable of destroying it.

The LORD would have to eliminate this hybrid species, and a natural force would be used for that purpose. It would have to be a force of great magnitude.

"But Noah found grace in the eyes of the LORD."

Noah was not only a good man and ethical in his conduct, but he and his family were "perfect in his generations." That means down through the generations, from Adam to his son Seth, through to Enoch and eventually to Noah and his sons, there was still a lineage of genetically unadulterated Homo sapiens. They had remained true to their spiritual advisor, the LORD of heaven, and had not married any of the daughters of men, no matter how fair they may have been.

"And Noah walked with God."

Noah was the patriarch of that small nation and the father of that generation. He was a prophet and a seer and communicated with the LORD via dreams, visions, prayers and meditations, and he heard the thoughts of God in his mind and soul. Noah, his LORD, and God were as one.

> *And Noah begat three sons, Shem, Ham, and Japheth.*
> *The earth also was corrupt before God, and the earth was filled with violence.*
> *And God looked upon the earth, and, behold, it was corrupt; for all flesh had corrupted his way upon the earth.*
> *And God said unto Noah, The end of all flesh is come before me; for the earth is filled with violence through them; and, behold, I will destroy them with the earth.*
>
> Genesis 6:10–13

The thoughts of God came through to Noah and he observed the scene around him. All was not well with his people. They were corrupt, immoral, and were exploiting their natural resources. All flesh—humankind and animal—was at risk, and even the earth had become corrupt. Noah had a premonition that the nation was about to be annihilated, and that it would happen soon.

Whether this predicted catastrophe was strictly a result of nature taking its course without human interference, or whether the people were instigating a destructive force, we will never know; but the Bible does suggest that the "earth is filled with violence *through* them." Could it have been a nuclear or atomic force that corrupted all flesh in that area?

From the beginning of the modern man there were giants and men of renown, and there were visitors from other worlds with advanced knowledge of the sciences. Add ego to knowledge without wisdom and one has a ticking time bomb.

Some of the knowledge these people had acquired may not have evolved within them naturally over time. Evolution is exceedingly slow and indirect.

The Homo sapien would have had help and information from an outside source, but it was like giving a baby a hand grenade to play with. In that period of time, we were still babes among the sons of men in the cosmos.

> Now therefore fear the LORD, and serve him in sincerity and truth: and put away the gods which your fathers served on the other side of the flood.... .
> Joshua 24:14

In the Bible, the word *gods* (lowercase g) refers to the ancient peoples' worship of idols made of wood or stone, the worship of the physical over the spiritual, and the worship of the strange men or women from the skies, whom they presumed were their gods.

> *Make an ark of gopher wood; rooms shall you make in the ark, and shall pitch it within and without with pitch.*
> *And this is the fashion which you shall make it of: The length of the ark shall be three hundred cubits, the breadth of it fifty cubits, and the height of it thirty cubits. [450 feet long, 75 feet wide, 45 feet high]*
> *A window shall you make to the ark, and in a cubit [18 inches] shall you finish it above; and the door of the ark shall you set in the side thereof; with lower, second, and third stories shall you make it.*
> Genesis 6:14–16

The Ark

In the Bible, an ark is a box or container to hold and preserve something that is considered precious. It is not, in the ordinary sense of the word, a ship. In the book of Jasher (which I will speak of in Chapter Eleven), it was said that Noah was a ship builder by trade and, besides being the patriarch of his generation, he was also "the father of those who sojourned upon the great waters." The great waters, in the Bible, are not lakes and rivers, but rather oceans and seas. The thought of God came through to Noah that he would need to build an ark for the water in order to preserve his family and his possessions from what was to come.

This would not be a ship, but would be more like a home afloat on the water. It would have had excellent sewage, lighting, and heating systems. It would have had fresh water, cooking and food-storage facilities and, with all those beasts on board, a great deal of ventilation. It was more like a barn afloat than a home, and this family and their creatures of "every kind" were in this sealed crate—for a year?

At this point, it would be very easy to say that the story of Noah and his ark is complete nonsense—a fable—and beyond belief. Nevertheless, let's carry on and see how this interesting narrative actually ends.

The story of Noah, his ark, and the flood over the *entire* world *is* a fable, a myth, or whatever else one wants to call it. What we have read in the Bible for centuries has been misinterpreted.

> *And, behold, I, even I, do bring a flood of waters upon the earth, to destroy all flesh, wherein is the breath of life, from under the heaven; and everything that is in the earth shall die.*
> *But with you will I establish my covenant; and you shall come into the ark, you, and your sons, and your wife, and your sons' wives with you.*
> *And of every living thing of all flesh, two of every sort shall you bring into the ark, to keep them alive with you; they shall be male and female.*
> *Of fowls after their kind, and of cattle after their kind, and of every creeping thing of the earth after his kind, two of every sort shall come to you, to keep them alive.*
> *And take unto you of all food that is eaten, and you shall gather it to you; and it shall be for food for you, and for them.*
> *Thus did Noah; according to all that God commanded him, so did he.*
>
> Genesis 6:17–22

The Flood of Waters

"Noah walked with God;" he listened to his feelings and he knew in his soul what he should do and how he should do it. He knew that the earth he was standing on would soon be destroyed and he knew that only he and his family would be saved because they were what remained of the perfect generations. The ark would keep them alive and allow them to begin again. The covenant of God would be for them.

It goes without saying that in the event of a flood of such magnitude, all living and breathing creatures will drown. Because Noah knew that a major portion of the land would be under water, he felt that he must save some of the animals. Naturally, a pair of each would be essential, but with limited space Noah would need to be selective of the species in the region. He left the door of the ark open because he knew that "two of every sort shall *come to you.*" He gathered enough food for them and his family.

I had pet hamsters for my children when they were young, and because of the hamster's mere two-year lifespan we had many of the cute little things through the years. These little critters were easy to tame and became part of the family in no time. Every evening after my kids were in bed, I would let the hamster out of its cage to run around the room and explore for a little while. One of our hamsters never did get tame, no matter what we tried, and that little one was not so easy to coax back into her cage for the night. I was forced to revert to mental telepathy. While she scampered around the room, I sat in a comfortable chair and visualized her going toward her cage and crawling in. I repeated the scene over and over in my mind and within five minutes she would be nestled in her cotton-lined cocoa tin bed.

I would use the same technique on my budgie birds and, on occasion, with my children, but with my kids it was not always successful. If I can use mental persuasion, I am sure that Noah would have been far better at it than I was.

He did not have to gather the animals together—they came to him.

What Noah did *not* do was round up every living creature in the world. Illustrations show, and stories relate, the animals going two by two into the ark: lions, tigers, giraffes, elephants, bears—you name it. Noah did build himself a big floating house, but it was not so large that he could fit the world's creation into it. That is what a fable consists of, and yet, through the centuries and to this day from the pulpits of the world, a biblical misinterpretation is promulgated as truth.

Tell me—how would Noah acquire two penguins from the Antarctic, and a pair of polar bears and walruses from the Arctic? How long would a kangaroo survive in a houseboat—or a giraffe—or a camel? Can anyone picture two elephants trying to keep their balance while being rocked to and fro on tumultuous waves? (At that time, there would have been mammoths with 4 metre long tusks). And think of all these animals together—the herbivores and the carnivores—with a couple of cobras in their midst. Not a pretty picture!

It has always been taught and preached in the churches and synagogues that this particular flood covered the entire world, and that is because our world believes that our planet is *earth*. In the Bible, earth is the word used for *all* that is made of matter, and all that is physical is, therefore, earthly. In science also, all that is matter is earth and all that is in the cosmos is earth. Our tiny, insignificant world is only a speck of dust of the earth.

In the Bible, "the face of the earth" was one particular spot or area and not the whole world or universe. In ancient times, writers would refer to the region that they were living in as their world, just as we sometimes do today.

In the New Testament, Peter speaks of the flood of Noah in a way that makes it seem like the entire planet was covered in water. He may or may not have known how big the world really was, or he might have just been referring to the world of the Adamic nation.

> ...That by the word of God the heavens were of old, and the earth standing out of the water and in the water: whereby the world that then was, being overflowed with water, perished. 2 Peter 3:5–6

"...The earth standing out of the water and in the water."

Could Peter have known that the area where the biblical flood was located was actually an *island* standing within the water of the ocean, *but* standing up and above it? And when it sank into the ocean, it was overflowed with water and perished.

Peter had read the Torah (the Word of God), and knew that the heavens and the earth *of old* did not stay the same as they were created, but evolve over time.

And the LORD said unto Noah, Come you and all your house into the ark; for you have I seen righteous before me in this generation.
Of every clean beast you shall take to you by sevens, the male and his female: and of beasts that are not clean by two, the male and his female.
Of fowls also of the air by sevens, the male and the female; to keep seed alive upon the face of all the earth.
For yet seven days, and I will cause it to rain upon the earth forty days and forty nights; and every living substance that I have made will I destroy from off the face of the earth.
And Noah did according unto all that the LORD commanded him.
And Noah was six hundred years old when the flood of waters was upon the earth.
And Noah went in, and his sons, and his wife, and his sons' wives with him, into the ark, because of the waters of the flood.
Of clean beasts, and of beasts that are not clean, and of fowls, and of everything that creeps upon the earth,
There went in two and two unto Noah and the ark, the male and the female, as God had commanded Noah.

Genesis 7:1–9

Early on, Noah had a premonition that disaster loomed, and that it had to do with water. The thoughts of God came through to him that he had to save his family and possessions by building an ark that could withstand the water.

Now, in Genesis Chapter Seven, Noah is communicating with the LORD through prayer and meditation and receiving answers to his questions via dreams. From the LORD, he learned how to prepare the ark with the necessities that would sustain life for all in the ark. One can communicate with God only through the process of thought and prayer, but a LORD speaks for God and as God would speak if we were able to hear him and see him.

Throughout the story of Noah and the flood, we read that Noah spoke and listened to God and the LORD interchangeably because, in essence, they are one. Because "Noah walked with God" he received his answers and messages through the process of thought and premonitions and through symbolic dreams and the still small voice that comes to us all. Most of us do not always listen, and do not hear. Noah knew how to listen.

Noah felt that he had to take in as many animals as he could look after because when the ark finally settled on dry land there may not be any animals in that particular area. He also felt that he had to have more than a couple of the "clean" species as food for them and some of the carnivores on board. A clean animal was usually a herbivore that these people could eat, in contrast to the unclean meat-eater. This was, and still is, a Semitic custom.

Before an earthquake, it has been observed that animals seem to have a sense of impending disaster; they get restless and appear to search for a safe place. Rats on ships, in earlier times, were seen leaving ships that docked, and that would be a warning sign for sailors that the ship's next voyage may be its last.

Perhaps there was a *feeling in the air* seven days before the rains came, and Noah did not have to chase around and collect the animals, especially the little wild ones that creep and crawl.

And it came to pass after seven days, that the waters of the flood were upon the earth.
In the six hundredth year of Noah's life, in the second month, the seventeenth day of the month, the same day were all the fountains of the great deep broken up, and the windows of heaven were opened.
And the rain was upon the earth forty days and forty nights.
And the flood was forty days upon the earth; and the waters increased, and bare up the ark, and it was lift upon the earth.
And the waters prevailed, and were increased greatly upon the earth; and the ark went upon the face of the waters.

Genesis 7:10–13, 18

And the waters prevailed exceedingly upon the earth; and all the high hills, that were under the whole heaven, were covered.
Fifteen cubits (22.5 feet) upward did the waters prevail; and the mountains were covered.
And all flesh died that moved upon the earth, both of fowl, and of cattle, and of beast, and of every creeping thing that creeps upon the earth, and every man.
All in whose nostrils was the breath of life, of all that was in the dry land died.
And every living substance was destroyed which was upon the face of the ground...and Noah only remained alive, and they that were with him in the ark.
And the waters prevailed upon the earth an hundred and fifty days.

Genesis 7:19–24

In the ancient Jewish calendar, the seventeenth day of the second month is equal to our months of April/May, and a time of gathering the first fruits of the season. It would have been a good time for Noah to stock the ark with nutritious substance.

That same day (the seventeenth), "were all the fountains of the great deep broken up, and the windows of heaven were opened." The *great deep* in this verse is the depth of the ocean. *This was an earthquake!* The earthquake was in the ocean, and the ocean floor was broken up, which caused the water (fountains) to rise into huge tidal waves, and what is called *tsunami waves* came up over the coastal land nearby and "the windows of heaven were opened." This was not just a rain, but a torrential burst of water that made it appear that the sky had opened up.

Where did this happen? The last time we looked in on these people their still small nation was situated in Eden where their ancestors originated. Over the millennia they must have wandered eastward, as did Cain in his time, and reached the shores of what is now the Gulf of Oman, and perhaps even as far as the Arabian Sea. Noah was a ship builder and "the father of those who sojourned on the great waters." Somewhere in this area or in the Arabian

Sea, there may have been an island large enough for a nation of highly civilized people. This island would have enabled them to experiment and *play* with the energy of Mother Nature—much like we read of what happened in the legend of Atlantis.

This, however, was not Atlantis. This *earthquake* happened approximately 1656 years after the Adamic race began; that I would say was in the range of 190,000 years ago. The massive destruction sank the island when the deep was broken up and all of its mountains and hills were covered. Nothing that breathed air remained alive, and even the coastal shores were washed clean of all life when the tidal waves inundated the land.

No ordinary flood on earth ever has, or ever will, cover the mountains. This could only happen if the earth sinks to the bottom of the ocean during an earthquake. This was no flood of just rain from the clouds, and this was *not* a flood that covered the whole world. The planet is round. When it is day on one side of the world, it is night on the other side. When it was the seventeenth day of the second month in Noah's region, and raining, it was snowing somewhere else and 35 degrees below zero. In another part of the globe, there may have been a dust storm at the precise time of the deluge in the Arabian Sea.

The Bible does not say that this flood covered the whole planet. What it repeats over and over is the flood destroyed the *face* of the earth, meaning one part or one area.

David explains in Psalm 104:5–9, the forming of the world in its beginning, but what some have mistaken for Noah's flood:

> Who laid the foundations of the earth...You covered it with the deep as with a garment: the water stood above the mountains. At your rebuke they fled...You have set a bound that they may not pass over; that they turn not again to cover the earth.

In its beginning the planet was covered in water, like a garment, but we have been given assurance that it will never happen again. On the fourth *day* of creation, God set the planet in its orbit around its own sun, which causes its seasons and days and nights. It is now impossible to have the globe covered in water.

> *And God remembered Noah, and every living thing, and all the cattle that was with him in the ark: and God made a wind to pass over the earth, and the waters assuaged;*
> *The foundations also of the deep and the windows of heaven were stopped and the rain from heaven was restrained;*
> *And the waters returned from off the earth continually: and after the end of the hundred and fifty days the waters were abated.*
> *And the ark rested in the seventh month, on the seventeenth day of the month, upon the mountains of Ararat.*
> *And the waters decreased continually until the tenth month: in the tenth month, on the first day of the month, were the tops of the mountains seen.*
>
> Genesis 8:1 – 5

After the rain from heaven had been restrained, a wind passed over what had been the coast and helped to dry the land. The flood on the mainland began to drain back into the sea as "the waters returned from off the earth continually." There were no more earthquakes or tidal waves: the "fountains also of the deep and the windows of heaven were stopped. . . ."

The ark had floated inland and rested on the mountains of Ararat. On the far eastern coasts of both Arabia and Iran there are mountain ranges, and they may not have been very high at the time. As the water drained away, their tops were the first to appear.

It was one year, according to the Bible, that Noah and his boarders spent enclosed in the ark—a year in a box full of animals of every description could really test the faith of the most devoted Bible reader. There is so much detail written about what God and the LORD said, did, and commanded Noah to do. There is the exact time in months and days that this event took place, but there is absolutely nothing that explains how eight people cared for these animals for an entire year. Nothing is said about how the food was stored and kept fresh, about sewage, ventilation, water, light or heat.

The account of Noah and the flood is long and repetitive, and this leads me to believe that over the centuries, it was copied and recopied—with some passages eliminated and others added by Jewish scribes of tradition and religion.

And Noah went forth, and his sons, and his wife, and his sons' wives with him:

Every beast, every creeping thing, and every fowl, and whatever creeps upon the earth, after their kinds, went forth out of the ark.

And Noah built an altar unto the LORD; and took of every clean beast, and of every clean fowl, and offered burnt offerings on the altar.

And the LORD smelled a sweet savour; and the LORD said in his heart, I will not again curse the ground any more for man's sake; for the imagination of man's heart is evil from his youth; neither will I again smite any more every living thing, as I have done.

While the earth remains, seedtime and harvest, and cold and heat, summer and winter, and day and night shall not cease.

And God blessed Noah and his sons, and said to them, Be fruitful, and multiply, and replenish the earth.

And the fear of you and the dread of you shall be upon every beast of the earth...into your hands are they delivered.

Every moving thing that lives shall be meat for you; even as the green herb have I given you all things.

But flesh with the life thereof, which is the blood thereof, shall you not eat.

And surely your blood of your lives will I require; at the hand of every beast will I require it, and at the hand of man; at the hand of every man's brother will I require the life of man.

Whoso sheds man's blood, by man shall his blood be shed: for in the image of God made he man.

And I will establish my covenant with you; neither shall all flesh be cut off any more by the waters of a flood; neither shall there any more be a flood to destroy the earth.

I do set my bow in the cloud...

Genesis 8:18–9:6, 11, 13

> *And it shall come to pass, when I bring a cloud over the earth, that the bow shall be seen in the cloud:*
> *And I will remember my covenant, which is between me and you and every living creature of all flesh; and the waters shall no more become a flood to destroy all flesh.*
>
> Genesis 9:14–15

A Promise, A Covenant, A Rainbow

The last passages pertaining to the biblical flood demonstrate a discrepancy that could be the result of too many authors over a long period of time.

The final copy, as was the whole of the creation story, was recorded on the scrolls by ancient Hebrew scribes and scholars from the world of antiquity, and eventually it became the Torah: the book from God.

It was Shem, Ham, and Japheth, the sons of Noah, who would have kept the story alive and handed it down to their descendants, but over time a life becomes a legend with many colorful variations.

The Hebrew narrative is not without fault. In it is a Noah who builds an altar and sacrifices of every clean beast and every clean fowl an offering to the LORD. The LORD smells a sweet savour and said in his heart that he will never again destroy all flesh on the earth.

The custom of clean and unclean beasts and fowl, and the ritual of sacrificial altars and burnt offerings to the LORD was a Hebrew religious practice. From Adam to Noah and after there were, as yet, no Hebrews, and there were no Jews. Noah was not a Jew. All races and ethnic groups on our planet today came *after* Shem, Ham and Japheth and their descendants had spread out around the world.

I believe that someone with deep religious convictions, much later in time, added his interpretations onto the story of the flood and he may not have known that the world was round. According to him, the LORD had said that the seasons and day and night shall not cease while the earth remains and that he will never again destroy all flesh with a flood. Then he goes on to say that the dread of man shall be on every creature, when in the creation account God had given man *dominion* over his creation. There is a difference between dread and being taken care of. All animals were now edible in the words of this last writer, but the practice of the clean and the unclean is still observed today among some Eastern religions.

A promise was supposedly made to Noah and the generations to come that all life would never again be destroyed by a flood, and a symbol of that promise was a rainbow in the sky. Was there never a rainbow before this? Was this the first time Noah had ever seen a rainbow? Why was it a promise now, when it must have appeared in the clouds for the first time after the first rain on earth? It is words like these that fables are made of.

The original ancient journals of the patriarchs from Adam to Noah have decayed and vanished with time. All that we have now are copies of the story of creation flavored with Hebrew customs, rituals and religion. However, it is because of this one ethnic group that we have a glimpse into our misty past, and one that is probably the nearest thing to the truth than any other nation or people could ever have presented to the world. There was a divine reason for this.

The Noah story ends with a very human frailty in a man who was a patriarch and who walked with God. On top of a mountain, where his family now lived alone and isolated, Noah planted a vineyard. When the grapes grew ripe, he made himself some wine, got good and drunk, and lay naked in his tent. His sons had to drape a garment over their shoulders, walk backward into his tent and cover his nakedness. This passage has always made me wonder: could they not have just told their mother to go in and cover up the old boy?

And old he was. The Bible states that he lived another three hundred and fifty years after the flood, and when he died he was nine hundred and fifty years old, according to the calculations of that time.

> *And the sons of Noah, that went forth of the ark, were Shem, and Ham, and Japheth...*
> *These are the three sons of Noah: and of them was the whole earth overspread.*
>
> Genesis 9:18 – 19

The Land of Shinar

Cain, in his era, had gone east of Eden to a land called Nod and built a city with a hominid people in the area and with his hybrid children. Within that same region, the sons of God who married the daughters of men eventually settled. They became a nation of giants and men of renown who had more brains than morals and they corrupted their island near the coastline of Oman. When the island broke up and the tidal waves washed the shores clean of all life, these hybrid people, and all that they had accomplished, sank to the bottom of the sea.

Now the children of the three sons of Noah would have to start over again. Once more it was a perfect generation and they were all direct descendants of Adam and Eve. As they multiplied, they stayed together and the "whole earth was of one language and of one speech." (Genesis 11:1)

> *And it came to pass, as they journeyed from the east, that they found a plain in the land of Shinar; and they dwelt there.*
> *And they said one to another, Go to, let us make brick, and burn them thoroughly. And they had brick for stone, and slime had they for mortar.*
> *And they said, Go to, let us build us a city and a tower, whose top may reach unto heaven; and let us make us a name, lest we be scattered abroad upon the face of the whole earth.*
>
> Genesis 11:2–4

What these people may have looked like or what their language was we can only imagine. The climate in that part of the world now is quite warm and it might have been even hotter 200,000 years ago (I will stay with that number) and that would have given these people a dark complexion with black hair and brown eyes. From Adam to Noah and from Noah to Peleg, there was neither Jew nor Gentile, black nor white, but perhaps more the color of coffee and cream. All of these first Homo sapiens were of one race and one language and they preferred to stay that way. Until this time they may have been a group or a tribe of nomads that had slowly wandered down from the mountains of Ararat and found the lush plains of Shinar too good to leave. They had journeyed from the east to Shinar and this would put them back, or near, the home of their ancestors once again, in the land of Eden.

Here they settled down and built a city and a tower that would reach into heaven. Today we would refer to it as a skyscraper. I doubt very much if they had intended to try and reach the third heaven, but who knows.

> *And the LORD came down to see the city and the tower, which the children of men had builded.*
>
> *And the LORD said, Behold, the people is one, and they have all one language; and this they begin to do: and now nothing will be restrained from them, which they have imagined to do.*
>
> *Go to, let us go down, and there confound their language, that they may not understand one another's speech.*
>
> *So the LORD scattered them abroad from there upon the face of all the earth: and they left off to build the city.*
>
> *Therefore is the name of it called Babel; because the LORD did there confound the language of all the earth: and from there did the LORD scatter them abroad upon the face of all the earth.*
>
> *These are the generations of Shem: Shem was a hundred years old, and begat Arphaxad two years after the flood:*
>
> Genesis 11:5–10

The Tower of Babel

"And the LORD came down to see the city. . . ."

The spirit LORDS of the third heaven do not come down to earth to see what people are doing or to communicate with them in a physical way. We can only communicate spiritually through thought, prayer and meditation. This was not a LORD from heaven.

This LORD was a man who came down from another planet, with the authority from the LORD Jehovah perhaps, to keep watch over this renewed species of Homo sapiens.

> *"Let us go down and confound their language..."*

The LORD from the sky did not come down alone. They arrived in a spacecraft that the Bible referred to on a number of occasions as cherubim. How they managed to confuse the language of the people is not stated in the Bible, but in the book of *Jasher*, he wrote that Japheth had asked his father Noah if he could take his children and their children and go to the land of Shinar, and eventually his brothers and their children must have followed. The book goes on to say that "there arose a great strife" and they scattered upon the earth. Maybe the LORD and his crew had something to do with that great strife.

As the people separated in groups and families and went their own way, their dialects would change over time, and over the course of centuries and millennia there would be different languages and different skin tones in shades of brown, black, and white. That is what isolation and climate does in an evolutionary world of the plant and animal kingdom.

That would have been the natural process rather than suddenly everyone babbling incomprehensibly and then separating, as the Bible suggests. We must remember the lack of knowledge of nature that some of the writers had, and how that would have affected how the scriptures were written in that time period. Also, the biblical writers had a strong tendency to abbreviate where a longer explanation would have been more helpful, and other times they could be exasperatingly repetitive.

Humans are naturally a curious species and it would have been only a matter of time for this globe to get densely populated; we still have that desire to travel and see the world. As we mature as a species, we are also developing a desire to travel to the stars and meet our neighbors on the many waters.

Chronology

The length of time between the birth of Adam and the deluge of Noah was 1650 years by biblical calculations, and that seems reasonable and accurate.

Although these people had many children and lived exceedingly long lives, they would still have been a small enough population to destroy with the sinking of an island and a tidal wave over the mainland.

From the time of the flood to the scattering of this rejuvenated people during the life of Peleg (the sixth generation of Noah) was approximately 300 years, and that too seems reasonable. From there on, however, the chronology of the Bible is inaccurate. According to the Bible, Adam was born approximately 6000 years ago, and the flood was 2348 BC.

The discrepancy may be due to the word *begat*. In the extensive chronologies in Genesis, and later in the books of Chronicles One and Two, there are a great many *fathers* of tribes, cities and nations which they *begat*. The word does not necessarily mean the direct descendant of a certain person, and writers and translators in later years may have felt that they had to fill in the blanks with the ages and deaths of these fathers and patriarchs.

I find it difficult—no impossible—to accept a chronology so extremely accurate from a Hebrew nation that was constantly on the move, vanquishing one nation after another and being in almost constant captivity during its ancient history. Things can get lost in moving from one house to another, so consider what can happen with a nation over a few millennia.

Adam and Eve were born at least 200,000 years ago, if not more, and the flood was not much later than that. It is not likely that anyone will find pieces of the gopher wood from the ark. Nor would the bricks from the tower of Babel be found under a city later known as Babylon.

Babel: a city built by the first Homo sapiens who were "perfect in their generation."

> You are the Creator of the earth…of all that it brings forth…of the beasts and birds and of the shape of Adam and of the gene of his seed; and of the confusion of tongues and of the scattering of the peoples… .[1] (*The Dead Sea Scrolls: The War Rule*)

NOTES

[1] Vermes, G. (1962). *The Dead Sea Scrolls in English.* Middlesex, UK: Penguin Books, p. 137.

II
Jasher

THE *Book of Jasher* was one of the lost writings of the ancient Hebrews, but when it was discovered again after many centuries it was deliberately omitted from the King James Bible at the time of its compilation. Its existence and credibility was mentioned in the books of Joshua 10:13, and in 2 Samuel 1:18, and for generations it had been read, referred to, and preserved by the kings and princes of Judah. At the time of the Babylonian captivity, it was taken from the Jews and it disappeared.

Sometime within the century of 700 AD, Flaccus Albinus Alcuinus of Britain, Abbot of Canterbury went on a pilgrimage to the Holy Land to search for treasures and other *holy things*. With two companions who were well versed in the languages of the Middle East, they had traveled through several countries where they met an Ascetic who told them about a certain scroll that might be of interest to them. In Persia (Iran), in the city of Gazna, there was a scroll written in Hebrew called *The Book of Jasher*, an extant of the books of Moses.

Alcuin and his companions found the library where the manuscript was being preserved under lock and key and, after much persuasion and many payments of gold, they were allowed to come by every day and read the ancient writings. After more talks and more payments of gold they were given permission to come back and copy, and translate into English, the Hebrew manuscript, but only under the watchful eye of the custodian. At the end of every day it was again locked away. For the next three years they rented a house, lived and dressed like the people of Gazna, and translated the words of Jasher into English. No amount of gold could have purchased the scroll; it was not for sale.

In Alcuin's words:

> The Book of Jasher is a great scroll, in width, two feet, three inches, and in length, about nine feet. It is written in large characters, and exceedingly beautiful. The paper on which it is written is for thickness the eighth of an inch. To the touch it seemed as soft as velvet, and to the eye as white as snow. The ark it was in is of Mosaic work, finely and curiously wrought, but time and accidents have very much defaced the external ornaments of it.[1]

Together with this large scroll was a smaller one that explained who Jasher was.

Jasher was born in Goshen in the land of Egypt and was the son of Caleb—the General of the Hebrews while they were subjects of the Egyptians. During this time, Moses had escaped from his palace home of the Pharaoh and was living in Midian with his wife and sons, and his father-in-law Jethro—the priest and patriarch of Midian.

Before the exile of the Israelites from Egypt, Caleb had trained the young Hebrew men for war and eventually to lead the people out of the country. When Moses returned to Goshen, Caleb's young son Jasher was chosen by Moses to be the caretaker of his *rod*. Throughout the communications between Moses and the Pharaoh, Jasher would carry the rod for Moses and his brother Aaron, for it was the rod that was used to show the King of Egypt what the God of the Hebrews was capable of doing. Jasher became a constant companion to Moses during the life of the patriarch and knew him very well.

After the deaths of Moses, Joshua, and his father Caleb, the people of Israel made Jasher their leader and judge because he was known for his truth and uprightness, and was called *the upright man*. When Jasher was near death, he passed his scroll onto his eldest son Jazer who then built the ark of gopher wood to preserve it for generations to come.

There are references to the *Book of Jasher* in the Old Testament, but it was not included in the canon—why not?

It may have been because his style of writing was in sharp contrast to the authors of these books, and especially to those attributed to Moses.

I believe, however, that all readers who have a scientific or historical interest in the biblical past should have access to another dimension of these ancient people's lives. What follows in this chapter will upset and disturb some people, but truth can sometimes have that effect.

Jasher did not write as one who was inspired or as one who wrote *what the Lord had commanded* of him. He engraved his thoughts onto his scroll as any journalist would: no symbols, no allegory and no poetics, just the facts as he experienced them.

Only the words of those that spoke and wrote as "they were moved by the Holy Ghost" were chosen to be included in the *Word of God* by those who compiled the Bible. But what is true inspiration and what is not? We know only too well of the atrocities that have been committed in the past, and still are on a daily basis, in the name of God or with God's blessing. The Bible is no exception.

The Old Testament is saturated with what God was supposed to have said, or what the LORD commanded. What was attributed to the deity was often ridiculous or even beyond human endurance, and one example of that is in Genesis 22:1 – 13: God tempted Abraham to offer his only son as a sacrifice. He was to murder Isaac and place the boy's body on the flaming altar like a chunk of meat to prove to God that he really was loyal and *feared* him.

The Bible does not record the words of Sara, but Jasher writes in chapter 3:20: "And Sara spake unto Abraham, and said, The holy voice hath not so spoken, for remember thou the words of that voice which said unto thee, I will make of thee a great nation." One has to agree with Sara. Not all *voices* are from God. God is not a homicidal maniac. He does not murder, strike anyone dead or instruct anyone to kill. He does not tempt anyone to sin or commit an evil act.

God the Conscious Energy and Light is Pure Love. Everything was created with Love, and when it was finished it was all "very good."

Down through the centuries, unquestioned reverence to everything that is in the Bible has replaced reason, and we seem to have lost the ability to discern what are the thoughts of God and what are the thoughts of men who are made of clay.

Perhaps a glimpse into the life of Jasher, the forgotten patriarch, will help us all to face reality and better understand the book that we refer to as the *Word of God*. Because it was written with human hands and human hearts, it contains sand and debris that has to be sifted to find the Word that in the beginning was with God, and *was* God.

Jasher begins his scroll with the story of creation, as told to him by his grandfather, his father Caleb, and his mother Azuba.

> Whilst it was the beginning, darkness overspread the face of nature.
> And the ether moved upon the surface of the chaos.
> And it came to pass, that a great light shone forth from the firmament, and enlightened the abyss.
> And the abyss fled before the face of the light, and divided the light from the darkness. . . .
> And the ground brought forth grass: the herb yielding seed, and the fruit-tree after his kind.
> And every beast after his kind. . . .
> And the waters brought forth the moving creatures, after their kind.
> And the ether brought forth every winged fowl, after his kind.
> And when all these things were fulfilled, behold JEHOVAH appeared in Eden, and created man, and made him to be an image of his own eternity. . . .
> And all the days of the life of Adam, there was rest, and peace, and quiet, unto all men.
> For they listened unto all things, concerning which he spake unto them. . . . Jasher 1:1–4, 7–11, 21–22

> And Lamech, the son of Methuselah, begat Noah.
> And Noah was the first who builded the ship: and who sojourned upon the great waters.
> And he was the father of those who go down into the deep, and who occupy themselves in much water.
> At this time the whole was of one lip, and of one word: and there was peace unto all.
> And it came to pass, that men were multiplied before the face of the earth; and they became mighty, and men of renown.
> And Japhet, and his sons, and his sons' sons, said unto Noah, Behold, thou art our father! Permit us, we beseech thee, seeing the land is not able to bare us...to pass over and dwell in the land of Shinar.
>
> Jasher 2:1–6

> And Noah said, Be it unto you, as ye list: only this thing I command ye, that ye worship the God of your fathers, observing all things which ye have received. . . .
>
> And from these men of renown rose up great nations, by whom the isles of the Gentiles were peopled. Jasher 2:7, 9

Jasher does not tell about the six days of creation or how God rested on the seventh day. As a matter of fact, God isn't even mentioned throughout the whole creation process. It all just "came to pass. . .that a great light shone forth. . .things were formed. . .and appeared. . .and the ground brought forth. . . ." And then, JEHOVAH appeared and formed the man.

There is no mention of the garden of Eden, the making of Eve, the murder of Abel or the building of the ark and the flood of Noah. And yet, the creation account is exact in its chronology to that of Genesis with all names accurate (except the spelling is different in some) and their proper settings.

The subject matter that Jasher omitted from his scroll may not have been known to the Israelites of Goshen, as they were slaves in Egypt and removed from the Jewish mainstream. However, if he did know the Genesis account he may have chosen to leave it out for the sake of brevity or because of the symbolic connotations that he may not have understood. Then too, it was his nature to recite only the basic facts.

Jasher goes on to write, in his own words, about the birth of Moses and their lives together during the exile from Egypt. He does not indicate if it was Moses who told him about his (Moses) unique birth, but Jasher's account is quite different from the biblical narrative.

> These are the words of Jasher, the son of Caleb, by Azuba.
>
> And it came to pass in process of time, that the children of Israel were multiplied exceedingly. . . .
>
> And Pharaoh was greatly vexed, and he said, This people will eat us up; wherefore ye shall slay every male of the Hebrews that cometh out of the womb, in the day that he is born shall he surely die.
>
> Now when the daughter of Pharaoh heard of these things she sought to turn away the evil imaginations of her father against the males of the children of Israel. Jasher 5:1–2, 6

And it came to pass that Moses the son of Amram, by Jochebed his wife, was the first male that came out of the womb after the decree of Pharaoh, king of Egypt, to slay all the males of the Hebrews.

And Jochebed the mother of Moses, with Miriam his sister, came unto Pharaoh's daughter; and Jochebed said, Behold here the son of thy handmaid!

And Pharaoh's daughter said, What wist you?

And they said, Thy father hath commanded that this infant be slain; yea, and that all the Hebrew males as soon as they are born be slain also.

And Pharaoh's daughter said, Give unto me the child. And they did so. And she said, This shall be my son.

And it came to pass, that the wrath of Pharaoh was turned away from slaying the males of the Hebrews.

And the child Moses grew and increased in stature, and was learned in all the magic of the Egyptians. Jasher 5:7–14

It is interesting to note that in Jasher's story of the birth of Moses there was no baby in a basket in the bulrushes.

ooo

In the land between the rivers, just west of the Persian Gulf, modern mankind was born and nurtured in the place called *Eden*. In the process of time, Noah's descendants settled back into this same area, then known as *Shinar*. Layers upon layers of civilizations flourished and then waned throughout the millennia, and then there arose from the rubbles of the past a civilization called *Sumer*. From these people were born mental giants and men of renown who could create, invent and build. From them also came writers, historians and poets who had stories to tell—legends and epics from their misty past that correlated with, *and were*, the beginnings of Genesis.

In the Jewish legend, the book that was given to Adam by the *angel* Raziel, and later became known as the *Book of Enoch*, was passed down from patriarch to patriarch. However, it remained only with the direct lineage from which the Lord of Lords would eventually come: from Adam to Seth, to Noah, to his son Shem, and on to Abraham, the father of the Semites. Noah's other two sons, Ham and Japheth, carried memories and stories passed down from them to their generations all around the globe. Memories faded with time, and the stories became legends and myths that were either embellished or completely erased. That is why today we have similar tales of the creation story, of the deluge, and of gods from the sky who reigned supreme.

The Book of the Generations of Adam (Genesis 5:1), was added to, and copied and recopied over and over again down through the millennia. Today we call it the Bible. It evolved along with the human species on this planet and, like us, it is still evolving.

In the retained memories of Sumer, the god *Enlil* in the beginning separated the heaven and the earth that had been born of the waters. He then came down and taught the first people agriculture and gave them tools. There was a deluge at one point and *Shuruppak* was ordered to build a ship because "the wide land would be shattered like a pot…overtaking the people like in a battle… ." (An earthquake)[2] Could Shuruppak have been Noah?

Over time the brick was refined by fire, and ziggurats were built to reach heaven, and the people began to argue, and had differences of opinion, and soon they spread out over the globe. They developed their own languages and cultures, and their isolation and the climate where they settled changed their features and the color of their complexions.

Thousands of years passed. How many? One can only guess, but more than Genesis was likely to have recorded, and more than our archeologists have been able to uncover. In this land between the rivers, which the Greeks later called *Mesopotamia*, there arose cities of advanced knowledge and cultures that have been greatly underestimated by our contemporary historians. In cities like Babylon and Ur, the most famous state of Sumer and home of Abraham, the people knew more of the mysteries of science than we have given them credit for, and Assyria had a large library of Sumerian writings collected by warrior kings of the land. One of these warrior kings, made into a legend, was Sargon, whose birth was celebrated with a poem:

> Sargon the mighty King, King of Akkad, am I.
> My mother was a changeling, my father I knew not.
> The brothers of my father loved the hills.
> My city is Azupiranu, which is situated on the banks of the Euphrates.

> My changeling mother conceived me, in secret she bore me.
> She set me in a basket of rushes, with bitumen she sealed my lid.
> She cast me in the river which rose not over me.
> The river bore me up and carried me to Akki, the drawer of water.
> Akki lifted me out as he dipped his ewer.
> Akki...appointed me as his gardener, Ishtar granted me her love.
> And for four...years I exercised Kingship.[3]

Note the similarities between Sargon and Moses. Sargon exercised kingship, and that may mean that he wasn't born into royalty. He just took over and made himself a ruler. Moses was brought into Egyptian royalty and later ruled his own people like a king and a leader. Both men were warriors and conquered nations. Moses was a ruthless leader in the name of God and the LORD for the children of Israel.

Sargon's mother was a changeling (a simple woman). Moses's mother was a slave in Egypt. Sargon didn't know his father, and Moses probably didn't know his father too well either, as he was brought up in the palace of the Pharaoh. Sargon knew where he came from and who his father's people were. His people lived in the hills and loved their freedom of nature, which probably meant that they were nomadic. Not all of the Jewish tribes were slaves in Egypt, only the children of Israel whose father was Jacob. The brethren of the father of Moses were free nomads in the surrounding hills of Mesopotamia and Arabia.

Sargon's mother bore him in secret. Moses's mother had to deliver him in secret and without a midwife because they had been ordered to kill all Hebrew males at birth. Sargon was placed in a basket lined with bitumen and placed in the river amongst the rushes and so was Moses. According to the Bible, Sargon was raised by strangers, and someone granted him her love. Moses was adopted by the Pharaoh's daughter who loved him as her own son. Sargon doesn't say whether Ishtar was his mother or his lover.

Both Sargon and Moses were Semites. Was the birth of Moses later embellished by a scribe to compare him to Sargon—a self described King, or was it that Sargon was actually Moses? Why was Jasher's account of the birth of Moses so different from that in Genesis when he may have received the information directly from Moses? Unless we find more ancient writings buried in the yet unknown caves, these questions will remain unanswered.

Moses was an extraordinary man, no question about that. His life was saved at birth under circumstances that were unusual whether he'd been plucked from the bulrushes or not. He grew up in wealth and splendor, and was granted the best education the world had to offer at that time. He was taught reading, writing and arithmetic, and also the magic that Egypt was well known for.

Moses had always known that he was a Hebrew and not an Egyptian, and that his people in Goshen were oppressed captives of the present-day Pharaoh. Jasher tells of how Moses fled from Egypt into the land of Midian (Saudi Arabia) when the Pharaoh learned that he had stirred up the Hebrews to rebel against Egypt. In Midian, Moses lived with Jethro—the prince and priest of that land—for the next thirty-nine years; and during that time he married Jethro's daughter Zipporah and she bore two sons. While there, he tended Jethro's flocks and learned the history of his people, and of their God and their LORD.

> And it came to pass after Moses had fled from the face of Pharaoh, and had left his brethren in the land of Goshen,
>
> That Caleb, the son of Hezron, invented the bow: for he was a mighty man and a man of renown.
>
> He taught the children of Jacob to shoot with the bow: he learnt his brethren to prepare themselves for battle. Jasher 6:11 – 13

This passage about Caleb is not in the Bible, but it is probable that Moses, on returning to Egypt after the death of the Pharaoh who sought to kill him, would gather and enlist the young men of Goshen in preparation for exile. Caleb, Jasher's father, was the leader of this new army and had already trained the men for battle. *He invented the bow and arrow*! Until then, no army before this time, and least of all the Egyptians, had the use of bows and arrows. Apparently only swords were used in warfare, but the new weapon of the Hebrews far outweighed anything of the sort in the Egyptian army.

> And Moses spake unto the children of Israel, and said, Whilst I sojourned in the land of Midian, I heard a voice saying unto me: Arise, go up unto thy brethren, for I will by thy hand bring back the children of Jacob, and they shall possess the land of Canaan from whence they came out. Jasher 6:16

From this point on, Jasher and the book of Exodus in the Bible begin somewhat to part company. Jasher does not speak of a burning bush that was not being consumed or of the voice of God coming from the bush. And yet Jasher and his father Caleb were by now in regular contact with Moses and, after they had left Egypt, were by his side until his death.

> Now Moses kept the flock of Jethro his father-in-law, the priest of Midian: and he led the flock to the backside of the desert, and came to the mountain of God, even to Horeb.
> And the angel of the LORD appeared unto him in a flame of fire out of the midst of a bush: and he looked, and behold, the bush burned with fire, and the bush was not consumed.
> And Moses said, I will now turn aside, and see this great sight, why the bush is not burnt.
> And when the LORD saw that he turned aside to see, God called to him out of the midst of the bush, and said, Moses, Moses. And he said, Here am I.
> And he said, Draw not nigh hither: put off your shoes from off your feet, for the place where you stand is holy ground.
> Moreover he said, I am the God of your father, the God of Abraham, the God of Isaac, and the God of Jacob. And Moses hid his face; for he was afraid to look upon God.
> And the LORD said, I have surely seen the affliction of my people which are in Egypt. . . . Exodus 3:1–7

By Jasher's account, Moses just heard a voice. Maybe that was all that Moses had told him, or maybe it was all too deep and mysterious for Jasher to repeat in his own narrative of his life with this great man. The Exodus story of the burning bush, however, is not at all far-fetched and is not beyond the reality of today's knowledge of electronics. The scientific knowledge that we have now was thought of as miracles in those days, and even in the early years of AD.

"And the angel of the LORD appeared to him in a flame of fire out of the midst of a bush. . . ."

The *angel* that Moses saw was a *human* messenger sent by the LORD Jehovah, who was the *God* of Abraham, Isaac, and Jacob, but *not* God the

Creator: the Supreme Being. Had it been God the Creator, he would also have been the God of the Egyptians. The messenger of the LORD spoke to Moses for the LORD, and as the LORD would speak to him on a personal level. The messenger, whom Moses thought was an angel of the LORD (and in a sense he was), appeared to him from out of the midst of a burning bush.

The bush, however, was not really burning. It just looked like it was because something behind the bush was likely very bright with colored lights that pulsated and flashed, and was like something Moses had never seen before (later in his life he would become familiar with cherubims). When the messenger noticed that Moses was coming too close to the bush, he warned him to keep his distance. Why? Radiation?

In the Bible's book of Exodus, Moses got his first visitation and received his first instructions from the LORD Jehovah through a human messenger from an advanced planet who guided Moses and his people *physically* throughout their exile from Egypt. The LORDS of heaven do not appear to humans in physical form, nor do they travel around the universe in spaceships, or in this case—cherubims. Only the sons of men from the many waters can do that.

During his youth, Moses had learned the sciences and the magic of Egypt. As an adult, he would learn the mysteries of the Spirit of God from his mentor and father-in-law, Jethro. Now in his old age (80 years), he was called on to perform a stressful and strenuous task that would require all the knowledge of both Egypt and Midian, and all of his physical endurance. Someone from a planet with a greater mental and spiritual knowledge had to help Moses and prepare him for his new venture.

His people were a special group of the sons of men on this planet, and they needed to be cared for and guided like no other race or ethnic nation in our world. From this wayward, stubborn, and child-like nation would eventually come a man who would teach this planet, once again, about the *rest* of God, and the kingdom of heaven that is within each and every soul.

Moses was a man of God, a prophet, a seer and a magician all wrapped up into one body. He led his people with the words of the LORD, and kept them on the straight and narrow throughout his lifetime. However, when we read the words of Jasher we also see that Moses was a ruthless warrior and a blood-thirsty dictator, and today he would be labeled a zealot who practiced genocide on a near-continual basis, and all in the name of the LORD, of course!

Maimonides, the Jewish philosopher of the Middle Ages, once explained the nature of prophecy:

> He said that the prophet is, first, a man of perfect ethical conduct; second, of great intellectual attainment; and third, blessed with tremendous fantasy. But even these attributes do not by themselves make the prophet...[he] must also be touched by the spirit of God...depending on how the spirit of God manifested itself to him.
>
> The lowest degrees of prophets were those who merely felt the need to speak out...The next levels included those who received their prophecies in dreams...On the highest level were those like Abraham who saw visions while awake. These classifications cover all prophets except the Prophet, Moses. He was alone in having direct communication with God, which allowed him to bring the Torah to man.[4]

Maimonides had the mistaken belief, as many religious people still do now, that Moses had personal contact with God the Creator and Supreme Being. It is a common and well-entrenched belief that Moses was together with God on the holy mountain of Sinai.

Once again...no human, no angel, no invisible from the heaven of heavens, and not even the Son of God, the LORD of all LORDS has heard God's voice or seen his shape. God is invisible. He is the Energy of all energy, the Light of all light. He is around all, above all, and through all.

The Bible says it was the *LORD*, the God of Israel who was on the mount with Moses. And yet, according to Jasher not even the LORD was there on that memorable occasion. Before Moses received the commandments, however, there was a departure from Egypt that had to be organized and Moses had to convince a Pharaoh to let his people go. Persuading a Pharaoh of Egypt would be a challenge, but Moses had the *rod* of God to help him.

> And Moses took his wife and his sons...and he returned to the land of Egypt: and Moses took the rod of God in his hand.
>
> Exodus 4:20

> And Moses said unto the elders of Israel, Send also with me Aaron, my brother, that he may be a spokesman for me, and for you. And also Jasher, the son of Caleb, that he may bear the rod before us.
> Jasher 7:2 – 3

The Rod

There were many kinds of rods referred to in the Bible—from the branch of a tree to an instrument of high voltage. Mostly, the rod was a measuring device much like the ruler of today and a symbol for the measure of justice, such as a code of ethics. "Spare the rod and spoil the child," for example, was not so much a command to beat a child with a stick, but to give the child a code of ethics to live by. Solomon, however, did say that the child will not die if beaten. That was then, and Solomon was not always right. He was human.

The rod of Moses and Aaron was not a measuring device, but an instrument that would probably resemble a laser today. It was a rod of energy and light that needed special handling and extra protection from misuse. The instrument was not common to the general public and was considered magic by the uninitiated.

Moses had been taught the magic of Egypt, and he may have acquired a rod early in his youth from the palace of the King. It could also be that while in Midian he received the rod from his father-in-law who was a priest, a patriarch, and a man of renown in his country.

True magic deals with the power of suggestion, and the magician knows how to manipulate what the observer perceives. To the people of the time, anything that was not understood was considered magic, a mystery, or a miracle. Actually, there is no such thing as magic, mystery or miracle; it is all within the universal law of Mother Nature, and the laws of nature cannot be broken. It is not good, nor is it evil—it just is.

Moses took the rod of God in his hand when he returned to Egypt to lead his people to freedom. He showed them what he could do with the rod and how it could be transformed into a serpent and the people were amazed at the wonders that he could perform in the name of God. He told them how the LORD, who was their God, would take them out of Egypt and lead them through the wilderness, and he would be the LORD'S spokesman—he and his brother Aaron, and Caleb's son Jasher, who would bear the rod for them.

Although the Bible never fully explains the power of the rod, the implications are that this was nothing less than a very important instrument for its time.

> Yea, though I walk through the valley of the shadow of death, I will fear no evil: for you are with me; your rod and your staff they comfort me. Psalm 23:4

> And there shall come forth a rod out of the stem of Jesse, and a Branch shall grow out of his roots...and he shall smite the earth with the rod of his mouth, and with the breath of his lips shall he slay the wicked. Isaiah 11:1–4

> And he shall rule them with a rod of iron.... Revelation 2:27

In one of the Aggadic tales of the Jewish Midrash, the Torah forbade Solomon to build his altar to God with iron tools. He went to the wise men and asked them how he could possibly build without the use of iron tools and they suggested that he search for the *shamir*. The shamir, they told him, is the "worm that cuts stone, [and was] used by Moses to engrave the names of the tribes on the gems that covered the breastplate worn by the high priest.[5]

> And the house, when it was in building, was built of stone made ready before it was brought thither: [at the quarry] so that there was neither hammer nor axe nor any tool of iron heard in the house, while it was in building. 1 Kings 6:7

(This was the house that Solomon built for the LORD that contained the cherubim so the LORD could communicate with him, mentioned in Chapter One)

In the Bible, it was called the *rod*, and Moses called it the *rod of God*. Jewish legend called it the *shamir*, and in ancient Peruvian writings it was the *vril stick* and was used to cut rock for buildings, monuments and *pyramids* that were then *levitated* into place! The levitation was either through electronic or mental power.

The wise men of Pharaoh's court were magicians who also had rods like the one Moses had, but according to Jasher, Moses could do more with his rod than they could. In the Bible passages of Exodus, the rod is not prominent in Moses's interactions with the King and it is the LORD who tells him always to stretch forth his hand to bring on a plague. Jasher, however, states that the Pharaoh was very interested in the rod and wondered why it could do more than the rods of his magicians.

The Bible states that the rod of Moses turned into a serpent on occasion. Jasher said that it was *as a serpent*, as were those of the King's court, but more so. There is a big difference between a serpent and *as* a serpent. It was a way of explaining a blast of light that appeared to coil around the rod—like a serpent.

After their escape from Egypt and their passing through the Red Sea, the people journeyed through the wilderness under the leadership and guidance of the LORD (Bible) and the Lord (Jasher). It is the same person except that Jasher did not use all capitalized letters when he mentioned the LORD, as was the custom of the Old Testament.

> And the LORD went before them by day in a pillar of a cloud, to lead them the way; and by night in a pillar of fire, to give them light; to go by day and night: He took not away the pillar of the cloud by day, nor the pillar of fire by night, from before the people.
>
> Exodus 13:21–22

> Then sang Moses and the children of Israel this song unto the Lord, and spake, saying, I will sing unto the Lord, for he hath triumphed gloriously: the horse and his rider hath he thrown into the sea.
>
> The Lord is my strength and song, and he is become my salvation: he is my God, and I will prepare him an habitation; my father's God, and I will exalt him.
>
> The Lord is a man of war: the Lord is his name… Who is like unto thee, O Lord, among the gods? Jasher 11:23–25, 33

One can see from both the Bible and Jasher's account of the exile that the LORD was not the God of heaven and earth. Only a physical being operates a pillar that is in a cloud by day, and lights up at night with flashing and pulsating lights that may look like flames of fire. This pillar was a vehicle, then known as a *cherubim*, and the LORD that communicated with Moses was a man. He was from an advanced civilization and under the direction of the LORD of heaven—Jehovah—the God of Israel. He too was called *God*, but he was a human servant and guide for the people, as was Moses.

From this pillar would also come the manna that was dropped from the sky every morning to feed the people until they could sustain themselves. Bible readers and scholars alike have always wondered about, and even searched for, a plant in the area that might have been what the Bible referred to as *manna*, but there was no plant of that nature. It is my theory that the manna was most likely a food supplement prepared in the cherubim.

Whether Moses actually knew the difference between God, the LORD of heaven, and the LORD in the spaceship, is uncertain, but throughout the Bible it appears that the patriarchs did know who they were dealing with. Moses called the LORD a "man of war: the Lord is his name." (Jasher 11:23–33). God is not a LORD and his name is not LORD; and he most certainly is not a man of war.

Moses at Mount Sinai

It came to pass when Moses had settled his people near the foot of the mountain of Sinai that his father-in-law Jethro paid him a visit. Jethro taught Moses how to distribute the many tasks and duties among the people and then, according to Jasher, Jethro said to Moses,

> ...after thou hast done all this, that thou shalt teach them laws and ordinances, that thou mayest direct them in the way that thy people should walk, and in the duties that they must do. Jasher 14:16

Jethro then established some commandments for Moses to give to the people, but when Moses's sister Miriam heard about it she objected and turned the people against Moses.

> And Miriam arose and said, Shall Jethro instruct the Hebrews? Are the children of Jacob without understanding?
> Are the customs of the Midianites to be brought in among us? Are we to forsake the good old paths in which our fathers, even Abraham, Isaac, and Jacob, have trod. Jasher 15:4–5

Moses became very angry with his sister and had her locked away and hidden, but the people protested against him because they held Miriam in high regard. He was outnumbered by the people and finally had to relent. After Miriam's death and the days of mourning were passed, Jethro came again to Moses "and Moses hearkened unto the words of Jethro his father-in-law: and he obeyed his voice in all that he had commanded him." (Jasher 16:3)

In the Bible, everything that Moses did and said was a commandment from the LORD.

> And Moses went up unto God and the LORD called unto him out of the mountain, saying, Thus shall you say to the house of Jacob, and tell the children of Israel… . Exodus 19:3

Moses was given every imaginable commandment, judgement and covenant in fine detail to present to the people. Also in exact detail were the instructions to build the Ark of the Covenant that was to house and protect the writings of the testimony, the mercy seat for communication with the LORD, and the tabernacle as a place for worship.

> And he said unto Moses, Come up unto the LORD, thou, and Aaron, Nadab, and Abihu, and seventy of the elders of Israel; and worship afar off. And Moses alone shall come near the LORD: but they shall not come nigh; neither shall the people come up with him. And Moses came and told the people all the words of the LORD, and all the judgements: and all the people answered with one voice, and said, All the words which the LORD has said will we do…Then went up Moses, and Aaron, Nadab, and Abihu, and seventy elders of Israel: And they saw the God of Israel: and there was under his feet as it were a paved work of a sapphire stone, and as it were the

> body of heaven in his clearness...also they saw God, and did eat and drink. And the LORD said unto Moses, Come up to me into the mount, and be there, and I will give you tablets of stone, and a law, and commandments which I have written; that you may teach them... . Exodus 24:1–12

In the following Bible verses there is evidence that Moses knew that he was not dealing directly with God the Supreme Being, but was talking to a fellow human being about the LORD of Israel—Jehovah:

> And the LORD descended in the cloud, and stood with him there, and proclaimed the name of the *LORD*. And the LORD passed by before him, and proclaimed, The LORD, The LORD God, merciful and gracious, longsuffering, and abundant in goodness and truth...And Moses made haste, and bowed his head toward the earth, and worshipped. And he said, If now I have found grace in your sight, O *Lord*, let my Lord, I pray thee, go among us; for it is a stiffnecked people; and pardon our iniquity and our sin, and take us for your inheritance... . Exodus 3:5–9

The LORD came down and stood with Moses and "proclaimed the *name* of The LORD, The LORD God, merciful and gracious... ." Moses in turn humbled himself before this LORD from the sky because he had come to him in the name of the LORD Jehovah, the God of Israel. Moses then referred to him as *Lord* because although he was doing the work of and for Jehovah, he was still a human like Moses. Moses said, "Let my Lord, I pray thee, go among us... ." What he is saying is that he (also a Lord) be allowed to continue to lead the people, and to pardon their weaknesses and keep them in God's inheritance.

Bible readers throughout the world know the Bible story of how Moses brought down the tablets of stone from Mount Sinai and the ten commandments that were written on them by *God*. These Ten Commandments, down through the ages, would be the cornerstone of this planet's justice system, its ethics, and its morality.

Jasher presents another side to the story. His words might cause some consternation among Christians and Jews alike, but keep in mind that Jasher was well known as a truthful and upright man who carried the rod before Moses, and later became ruler of Israel.

> And Moses said unto Nadab and Abihu, the sons of Aaron: Go to now, and build ye an altar, even as Jethro has dictated unto you.
> And Nadab and Abihu builded an altar nigh unto mount Sinai, even as Jethro had dictated: and they set up twelve pillars, according to the number of the tribes of the children of Israel.
>
> Jasher 16:4–5

> And in those days it came to pass, that Moses spake unto Aaron, and unto Hur, saying:
> Stay ye with the people here, and judge them, for lo, I shall go up on the mount with Joshua, Nadab, and Abihu, and the elders; and we shall stay there forty days and forty nights.
> And I, Jasher, the son of Caleb, bare the rod before Moses and Joshua, and the seventy elders of the people. Jasher 16:12–14

> Now it came to pass on the morrow, that Jethro met Moses, Joshua, Nadab, Abihu, and the seventy elders, on the mount; and the trumpet sounded.
> And on the second day, about the ninth hour thereof, the trumpet sounded, and Jethro, Moses's father-in-law, stood forth and said:
> Behold, thus saith Jethro, the son of Esau, the priest of Midian: It is meet, O Israel! That ye build a tabernacle for the God, the maker of heaven and of the earth; *even* for the God of Abraham, the God of Isaac, and the God of Jacob, that ye may serve the Lord, who hath delivered ye out of the hands of the Egyptians, and from the dangers of the Red Sea.
> Then Jethro instructed Moses in what manner and in what form, and with what materials he should build the tabernacle of the Lord of Hosts.
> Moreover, ye shall build an ark unto the Lord, wherein ye shall lay up before the Lord the testimony; even the writings of the laws and ordinances which ye shall receive.
>
> Jasher 17:1, 4–5, 8, 12

> And it came to pass, when the forty days were fulfilled, wherein Jethro communed with Moses, Joshua, and the seventy elders, that all the statutes and the ordinances to be observed, were written in a book of remembrance. Jasher 17:13

When Moses escaped to Midian, it was Jethro who took him in and taught him about his people and about God. After the exile, it was Jethro who visited him and taught him how to be a leader of the people and how to govern them. It was Jethro again who came back later and gave Moses the ordinances, the statutes, and the commandments in the book of remembrance, for the ages to come. Jasher was there and observed them being written by Jethro in communion with Moses.

During the forty days while Moses and his elders were on Mount Sinai with Jethro, the people down at the foot of the mountain grew restless and resented the fact that Jethro was giving Moses the laws for them to observe when he was not of their tribe, but rather a Midianite. Aaron then sent a messenger to Moses and telling him that the people were getting rebellious and he was losing control. Moses sent back the messenger and became very angry. He held a meeting with Joshua, Aaron's two sons, and the seventy elders, and suggested to them that they tell the people that they had seen the Lord, and had eaten and had drunk with him, and that it was the Lord who had given the commandments to them.

> Behold, thus it behoveth us to say unto the people: We have seen the Lord in the mount, we have ate and drank in his presence, and the words which he hath spoken unto us, they are those which we now deliver unto you. Jasher 17:22

Everyone in the assembly agreed that this was what they should tell the people, except Aaron's two sons Nadab and Abihu. "And the saying of Moses was pleasing unto Joshua and the seventy elders: but unto Nadab and Abihu it was not pleasing." And Aaron's two sons were cut off from the assembly and had to leave. When they returned to the camp at the foot of the mountain, they told the people what had transpired, and the people became rebellious against Moses and his elders, but spoke well of Nadab and Abihu. (Jasher 17:23–27)

Then said Moses unto the sons of Levi...Gird on each man his sword, and go ye through the camp, and slay ye the froward, even every man his friend.
And they did so: and they slew Nadab and Abihu, the sons of Aaron, with three thousand of the people.
But Aaron held his peace.
And it came to pass, when the slaughter was over, that the children of Israel humbled themselves, and they said:
All that the Lord shall say unto us, that will we do.
And the people sent messengers unto Moses, and unto Aaron, and unto Joshua, and unto the seventy elders, saying:
We have done wrong; we have sinned; entreat ye for us.

Jasher 18:5–11

Moses knew that he would never have control of the people unless he put the fear of the Lord into them and used the name of the Lord to confirm his words and actions. From this point on in Jasher's account, Jethro is out of the picture, as in the Bible, and "*thus saith the Lord*" was the order of the day. Moses made himself the Lord's spokesman and whatever came from his mouth was from the Lord and whoever he raised his hand against was what the Lord had ordered. All who disagreed would be punished with death—they *and* their friends.

And when Korah, Dathan, Abiram, and On, with two hundred and fifty of the children of Israel, men famous in the congregation, and men of renown, saw all that was done,
They said one to another: This thing which Moses and Aaron have done, is not of the Lord. Jasher 21:1–2

And they gathered themselves together unto Moses, and they said unto him:
What thing is this that thou hast done? Are not all the people holy? Wherefore has thou separated the tribe of Levi, to be sanctified unto the Lord? Jasher 21:4–5

> And Moses said, Tomorrow shall the Lord answer the blasphemies you now utter: and show who is holy, and who is not holy.
>
> Jasher 21:7

> And Moses commanded the Levites, saying: Up now, slay Korah, Dathan, and Abiram, with those that are with them, with fire, even as the Lord has spoken unto me.
> And Korah, Dathan, and Abiram, with two hundred and fifty men of the children of Israel, perished by fire before the door of the tabernacle of the Lord.
> And great fear fell on all the congregation: and they hastened every man to his tent.
> Thus did Moses establish the priesthood in his brother's house, in the tribe of Levi: and he committed unto them, the keeping of the tabernacle, of the ark, and of the book of the testimony, according to all that the Lord had commanded him.
>
> Jasher 21:12–15

There were more than ten commandments. The people could barely keep up with all the laws, ordinances, covenants and commandments, so when they sinned (because it was near impossible not to) they had to make atonement by killing the best of their animals. All of this kept the tribe of Levi continually well fed and content—"Thus saith the Lord."

> Thus did Moses establish the feasts of the Lord; even as he was commanded on mount Sinai.
> Then came forth the son of Shelomith before the congregation, and spake unto Moses, at the door of the tabernacle, saying:
> The Lord hath not spoken these things; peradventure they are imaginations of evil to the people.
> And Moses commanded the Levites, saying, Lead him forth of the camp, and let the people stone him with stones, that he die, as the Lord hath spoken. Jasher 23:22–25

Jasher now speaks of the death of Moses:

> And Moses called for Eleazar, the priest, and he said unto him: Take now from Jasher, the rod, and do thou lay it up before the Lord in the tabernacle of the congregation, on the side of the mercy seat shall it be laid up.
>
> And I, Jasher, the son of Caleb, delivered unto Eleazar, the priest, the rod: and Eleazor put it up in the tabernacle, on the side of the mercy seat before the ark: and it remaineth there unto this day.
>
> And Moses died in the land of Moab.
>
> And Moses was an hundred and twenty years old when he died.
>
> Jasher 26:27–28, 32–33

And so ends the story of Moses as Jasher tells it. Moses was, and still is, considered to be the greatest of the patriarchs and prophets of the Old Testament. He was supposedly the only one who communed with God personally, and even dined with him. Jasher, throughout most of his life, walked with Moses, talked with him, and dined with him. Hour after hour, day after day, he was the messenger for Moses and the valet of his rod. Yet he never once saw God or even the Lord. Yes, he frequently wrote, "as the Lord commanded Moses," either because he believed in Moses or it was a way to save his own skin—he had seen what happened to those who doubted the words of this great man of God.

In the beginning of his leadership, Moses was sincere in his endeavor to lead his people into the promised land, and he may well have been in frequent contact with a Lord from the sky. In time, however, he learned that a "fear of the Lord" (the true meaning of the word) was the only thing that kept him in control, and his ego took over from there. He changed from being a man of God to a man of religion.

Laws and commandments were, and still are, necessary for humans in a civilized society. The Ten Commandments are basic, and this was what Jethro gave to Moses, along with a few laws, to keep the people in check and at peace. Where did Jethro get these commandments?

Jethro was a Midianite of the lineage of Esau, the twin brother of Jacob, the ancestral father of the Israelites. Like Jacob and their forefathers, he had access to the written knowledge of the ancients that had been handed down from patriarch to patriarch. Jacob and his sons, however, lived in Egypt on the invitation of the Pharaoh of the time, and later became slaves in their adopted country. During this time they may have lost their written heritage and only had what was handed down by word of mouth from the memories of their elders.

While Moses was in the land of Midian, he learned for the first time the revelation of God, as given in the beginning to Adam by Raziel. Down through the ages, the book of *The Book of the Generations of Adam* became the *Testimony* and *The Book of Remembrance*, and an ark was built to preserve it for posterity.

It was thought that Hammurabi, in the land between the rivers, was the first to draw up the world's legal code of ethics. We know now, however, that he may have had much earlier legal documents in the Sumerian language to draw from. A century and a half before Hammurabi, a code was discovered written by Lipit-Ishtar, ruler of the Dynasty of Isin:

> I, Lipit-Ishtar, the humble shepherd of Nippur, the stalwart farmer of Ur...established justice in Sumer and Akkad in accordance with the word of Enlil... ." (Enlil was the Sumerian name for God the Creator).[6]

When our planet first *arrived* and became one of the many waters, Adam was handed a code of ethics from Raziel; it was the *Word of God* for the universe, and now for our planet. Raziel was not an angel from heaven, but a man from one of our neighbors in the cosmos. Angels do not stop in for tea and give out books made of paper, or matter of any kind.

Eons of centuries later, the code of ethics that had been handed down in various forms was again presented on Mount Sinai in written form to humankind. It did not come from an angel, from a LORD from heaven, or from the hand of God. *God did not wine and dine with Moses.* It was given to our world by Jethro—a man who "walked with God."

ooo

I would like to personally thank the Supreme Grand Lodge, Rosicrucian Order, AMORC, San Jose, California, USA for presenting this ancient manuscript of *Jasher* to the world. It can only enlighten us in our quest for knowledge of the mysteries of the Bible.

NOTES

[1] *The Book of Jasher.* San Jose, CA: Supreme Grand Lodge, Rosicrucian Order, AMORC.

[2] Cottrell, L. (1962). *The Horizon Book of Lost Worlds.* New York, NY: American Heritage Publishing Co., p. 156.

[3] Cottrell, L. (1962). *The Horizon Book of Lost Worlds.* New York, NY: American Heritage Publishing Co., p. 134.

[4] Gersh, H. (1968). *The Sacred Books of the Jews.* New York, NY: Stein and Day Publishers, p. 193.

[5] Gersh, H. (1968). *The Sacred Books of the Jews* New York, NY: Stein and Day Publishers, p. 141.

[6] Cottrell, L. (1962). *The Horizon Book of Lost Worlds.* New York, NY: American Heritage Publishing Co., p. 153.

12
The Breath of God

> The Spirit of God has made me, and the breath of the Almighty has given me life. Job 33:4

WITH every breath we take we live a few seconds longer. Without a breath there can be no life. This is the law of the universe.

When the life that *is* God breathed into the blackness of space, the cosmos was born. She is our Mother Earth and through her we live and have our being.

She is nestled within the body of her Creator and each of the many waters is as an alveolus, a tiny pocket of air in the vast expanse of the universe. Without the worlds of life, she could not, nor would she have the need to, exist.

In our "brief history of time," earth has been expanding for billions of years, and when she has filled the universal diaphragm she will exhale for eons more. The time it takes for each breath is incomprehensible to us, but in eternity it is only a second.

All life on earth is born of her stardust, but matter is only a low vibration of energy and does not last. In the process of time, it grows old, deteriorates and decays, and earth will again be "without form and void" and there will be "darkness upon the face of the deep."

> Who has given him a charge over the earth? or who has disposed the whole world? If he set his heart upon man, if he gather unto himself his spirit and his breath; All flesh shall perish together, and man shall turn again unto dust. Job 34:13–15

We exist at this moment in time within the breath of God. It is the expansion of the cosmos. Someday, it will contract.

The Spirit and the Soul

Many writers and scholars of theology use the word *spirit* and *soul* as one and the same, and in a sense they are because they represent life.

The spirit is the divine essence of a living organism that gives it its personality and unique characteristics. All plants and animals are bathed in an aura of invisible light that is within and around every body and form that contains life. It is from the Spirit that moved upon the waters.

The "moving creature that has life," as the Bible describes the animal kingdom, has the additional ability to think, reason and feel emotions and pain, suited to its level of development. From the smallest insect to the largest of mammals, the process of *thought* is what sets it apart from the grasses, herbs and trees and gives it a spirit *and* a soul.

Thought cannot be explained by chemical analysis or seen in a test tube. We were animal. We evolved from animal and physically we still are animal. It is the process of thought that makes a mind and gives it consciousness and soul. It makes no difference whether the creature walks on two, four or six legs, or whether it has arms, wings or fins. We all have in us the same Beam of Light.

> ...the Receiver of the Light, purifies those powers...all the rulers gather together all matter...take it and fashion it into souls of men and cattle and reptiles and wild-beasts and birds, and send them down into the world of mankind.[1]

There has often been sharp criticism for people who give supposed human qualities such as love and benevolence to animals. In fact, all of our humanism originated in the animal kingdom. Take, for example, the *kiss*. Now and then, someone will speculate in the media on why people kiss and how it all got started. One has only to observe the animals. Most birds and mammals like to nuzzle and that is what a kiss actually is. It is an act of love. Ask any dog. *Dogs love to kiss.*

And how can the critics not see some of the disgusting behaviors that people have retained from their animal predecessors, such as biting and spitting and others that I won't even mention? We still have a way to go in our evolution.

As for benevolence, it even occurs within the world of insects, as I witnessed many years ago when I helped my daughter carefully lift an ant colony from the ground and place it into an aquarium. Of course, most of it was in shambles and the ants had to work hard at getting it back into order.

On the surface of the tank I noticed that one ant was trapped in a chunk of clay and was struggling. Two other ants came to her rescue and worked furiously to free her, but they couldn't. I took pity on them and, with a toothpick, I loosened the soil from around the tiny captive. The two would-be rescuers immediately checked over her entire body with their mandibles and appeared to clean her thoroughly. Then they stood back and waited for her to move and when she started to walk they went on their way to another task.

They seemed to have settled into their new home and I smeared a very thick coat of Vaseline around the top inside of the tank to keep them from wandering. Luckily, we left the aquarium outside overnight because in the morning when we checked on them, they were gone. They had built a bridge of dead ants a few layers thick, packed their belongings and moved out. Whether they had taken the bodies from their gravesite or whether some gave their lives for the cause, I'll never know. They did not leave a forwarding address.

> Go to the ant...consider her ways and be wise: which having no guide, overseer, or ruler, Provides her meat in the summer, and gathers her food in the harvest. Proverbs 6:6 – 8

The Living Soul

> And the LORD God formed man of the dust of the ground, and breathed into his nostrils the breath of life; and man became a living soul. Genesis 2:7

In the beginning of human evolution, man was of the animal kingdom. All hominids of different species and levels of intelligence were of the earth in spirit and soul. The spirit that permeates all life and the soul of the animal remains on earth and when the physical form can no longer sustain life, it departs and enters a new body. Life and its spirits and souls do not die. They are streams from the Light of God, and they reincarnate as long as the earth remains.

When the LORD God formed the first Homo sapien, he had to use the same material that harbors all life in the cosmos—from the dust of the ground. And the law of the universe dictates that all must breathe, for without breath there is no life.

Another law that cannot be broken is that all life on earth must begin in its infancy. Mother Nature is a nurturing and caring parent and she brings forth from her body only that which is fresh and new and has the potential to succeed. Even that which has been cloned from plant or animal has to sprout, hatch or be born. The first human on this planet was no exception.

The *living* soul, unlike that of the animal, is capable of knowing its origin, is able to understand and communicate with God and to grow in spirit and wisdom. It is not tied to the earth, but has its home in heaven.

Modern man was the final result of millions of years of hominid evolution and when his physical form and brain had reached the level where he could grasp the dimensions of good and evil and understand the consequences of his choices, he became one with his peers throughout the cosmos.

When baby Adam took his first breath of life in a delivery room in Eden, he was in "our image and likeness" and in the image and likeness of God, and he became a living soul.

> Hail to thee, Rã, Lord of Truth, whose shrine is hidden, thou Master of the gods, thou god Khepera in thy boat; at the going forth of thy word the gods sprang into being. Hail Atem, maker of mortals. However many be their forms, he nourisheth them, he maketh the color of one to be different from the other[2]

The Fruit of the Womb

Before any organism on earth can live it must breathe, just as the earth as a whole inhales and exhales with the breath of God.

When Adam took his first breath he *became* a living soul, and before that breath of life he was what the Bible refers to as "the fruit of the womb." He had no spirit and no soul, and he was "as if he had never been."

When Moses laid down the first laws and ordinances for the tribe of Israel he left nothing for speculation. The laws were very strict and the punishment was severe. The death sentence was often meted out for minor transgressions such as not honoring one's parents and if that were the law in our society today, we'd have few teenagers.

The fruit of the womb, however, was considered the property of the woman's husband and its value was based on what he thought it was worth.

> If men strive, and hurt a woman with child, so that her fruit depart from her, and yet no mischief follow [death or injury to the woman] he shall surely be punished, according as the woman's husband will lay upon him, and he shall pay as the judges determine. And if any mischief follow, then you shall give life for life, eye for eye, tooth for tooth, hand for hand.... Exodus 21:22–24

When Job was having his share of problems, he cried out to his LORD and cursed the day he was born:

> Why died I not from the womb? Why did I not give up the ghost when I came out of the belly?...For now should I have lain still and been quiet, I should have slept...Or as a hidden untimely birth I had not been; as infants which never saw the light. Job 3:11–16

> Wherefore then have you brought me forth out of the womb? Oh that I had given up the ghost, and no eye had seen me? I should have been as though I had not been: I should have been carried from the womb to the grave. Job 10:18–19

David speaks of the wicked in society:

> ...as a snail which melts away, let every one of them pass away: like the untimely birth of a woman, that they may not see the sun."
>
> Psalm 58:8

In our society, a woman and her body is no longer the chattel of her husband or anyone else. The fruit of her womb is hers alone and the value she places on it is at her discretion. If she decides to bring a damaged child into the world and she is to blame for the damage, her soul will bear the responsibility.

> But ask now the beasts, and they shall teach you; and the fowls of the air, and they shall tell you: Or speak to the earth, and it shall teach you: and the fishes of the sea shall declare unto you. Who would not know in all these that the hand of the LORD has done this? In whose hand is the soul of every living thing, and the breath of all mankind. Job 12:7–10

> And God saw everything that he had made, and behold, it was very good. Genesis 1:31

Like the pieces from a hologram, each and every *living soul* throughout the cosmos and in the heaven of heavens is the complete image and likeness of God. As he is God, so we are gods.

Because he is the Life of all life, the Spirit of the spirits and the Soul of souls, he has dominion over every breath we take. In like manner, we have been given dominion over the creatures with whom we share our lives and the world in which we live, and we have control over every breath *they* take.

> A righteous man regards the life of his beast: but the tender mercies of the wicked are cruel. Proverbs 12:10

The garden of Eden was a microcosm of how our planet was to be, and the planet was to be a holographic fragment of the paradise in heaven. The garden on earth was beautiful, serene and filled with fruitful trees and friendly animals and birds.

The trees of the world purify our air and keep us breathing and, therefore, it is only natural that a symbol for life would be a tree. All earthly life came from the ground and spread its branches into many forms and varieties and they in turn bore fruit after their kind.

The *tree of life* that was in the midst of the garden of Eden bore the fruit of wisdom for the living souls of humankind. As souls in the likeness of God, we have the capacity to understand the wisdom of being one with the Spirit and of being good and able stewards of our home on earth. As a matter of fact and truth, it is our duty and obligation to care for our global garden—"to dress it and to keep it."

A Taste of Evil

Our first parents were born of the dust of this planet and had gained the level of understanding the dimensions of God and the concept of good and evil. Unlike their hominid cousins, they had choices and they reached out and tasted evil.

> And God saw that the wickedness of man was great in the earth, and that every imagination of the thoughts of his heart was only evil continually. Genesis 6:5

Down through the millennia evil has ruled our world, but it did not begin with our first parents. Evil is the lowest and darkest part of God the Energy and the Light. The angels of heaven were created before the earth ever was and they were first to have the tree of the knowledge of good and evil in their midst. Some of the hosts of heaven chose evil.

> And the angels which kept not their first estate, but left their own habitation, he has reserved in everlasting chains under the darkness unto the judgement of the great day. Jude 6

> For if God spared not the angels that sinned, but cast them down to hell. . . . 2 Peter 2:4

It was the angels who sinned in the misty past who terrorized the ancient people of all races and nations, and are the original evil spirits and demons of legends and religions to this day. We are lower in power and vibration than the invisibles of heaven, and it was thought that a nasty angel could indeed wreak havoc on a human soul.

Lucifer was supposed to have been the archangel who led his host of angels into rebelling against the Lords of God and they were cast out of heaven and into the *pit*, which is lower in vibration than the earth. *Beneath the earth* was a description of hell that prompted people in the Middle Ages to think that hell was in the middle of our planet. Some may still believe that today.

The chief of all evil is Satan, and Satan has many other names to his credit. He is known as the *Devil*, *Beelzebub*, *Abaddon* (Hebrew), *Apollyon* (Greek), *the Dragon* and, of course, *the Serpent*. Many nations personified him as having the form of a human or reptile, but some, like the early Egyptians, pictured evil as grotesque animals with mix-and-match heads and body parts.

But what exactly *is* evil? Everything that exists and was created from God the Energy and the Light has dimension. In heaven and earth there is length and width, top and bottom, inside and outside, darkness and light. There is also dimension of the spirit and the soul, and that we refer to as our morals. It is the knowledge and the choice of good or evil.

The people of ancient times had to personify much of their thoughts and feelings in order to understand them. They had to have a mind picture and to *see* the abstract thought, and what better way than to make it into a human or animal form. It was fairly simple to think of evil as a snake or scorpion as they are not known for their good deeds or compassion toward their fellow creatures. Even today, we've put the devil in a man's body, but he has hoofs, horns and a pitchfork, ready and willing to torment us.

Although the writers of the Bible personified evil, if read carefully it is clear that they knew the difference between a spirit entity and a moral thought or deed. When Jesus relayed the message to his disciples that he would have to suffer and die, Peter assured him that it most certainly would not happen. Jesus turned to him and said, "Get thee behind me, Satan." (Matthew 16:23)

Evil is an imagination of the thoughts of the heart (soul) that is undesirable, harmful or destructive. It is a thought that can cause distress, injury or death to another innocent soul, or an act that results in suffering, misfortune or disaster. *There is no one called Satan*—no person, no angel, snake or scorpion. Evil is in each and every one who is a living soul. It lies at the very bottom, in the deepest, darkest part of the human psyche.

Hell

> Can you by searching find out God?…it is as high as heaven…deeper than hell… . Job 11:8

The Bible describes hell as being in the nethermost part of the earth and in utter darkness. It is also referred to as *the pit* or *the lake of fire* and, as I have mentioned, it was once believed by the Christian Church to be in the center of our planet. It was assumed that the core of our globe was on fire and extremely hot and, of course, in utter darkness. Where else could hell be?

Matter, in the Bible, is called *earth*, as is the cosmos. Does that mean that hell is in the middle of the universe—wherever that is? Hardly.

God is all there is. Everything that exists is from the Energy and the Light. It reaches to the height of forever in brightness and down to the lowest vibration and frequency of the darkest of the dark. "Nethermost part of the earth" means that within matter is a force from which matter was made. It is the core of earth and it is a *dead* force.

> Dead things are formed from under the waters, and the inhabitants thereof. Hell is naked before him, and destruction has no covering. He stretches out the north over the empty place, and hangs the earth upon nothing… . Job 26:5–7

From a living God there had to be dead matter that would accommodate life and give it body. "Dead things" (matter) were formed from "under the waters" (opposing forces of energy deep within the universe). Could that be what science refers to as antimatter? From the opposite forces of energy came the dust of the earth and formed the cosmos.

This lowest form of energy is of a destructive nature and that is why matter does not last forever. It was designed to last only during one breath of God.

"Hell is naked before him, and the destruction has no covering." Hell is the lowest level and the deepest and darkest part of God. Despite this, it is not hidden or covered, but an important and necessary force of the Energy and the Light.

Job thought of the universe as being a level higher than the place called hell, which is south of the universe. And God stretched out his northern area that was empty and set up the cosmos without anything to hold it in place.

The destructive forces of hell are necessary within the dimensions and nature of God. But just as a willful child is warned of the dangers that are otherwise necessary for the quality of life, such as fire, humankind is warned about the dangers of evil. "For in the day that you eat of it you shall surely die."

Our living souls come from the highest part of God. From his breath we were made conscious beings in his likeness and in his image and like him we are dimensional and have within us good and evil, and life and death. Hell to us is both a place and a condition of the soul. Only we can choose which way we want to live.

> The way of life is above to the wise, that he may depart from hell beneath. Proverbs 15:24

Crime and Punishment

> Whosoever sheds man's blood, by man shall his blood be shed: for in the image of God made he man. Genesis 9:6

Cain murdered his brother Abel. Why did he not have to die for his crime? He had feared for his life from the hominids in the area, but he was spared by the *mark* that was on him, and by the fact that there were no other humans to pass judgement. The LORD God and his people had left the planet long before. Sure, there were his parents, but they were nice people and hardly expected to be his executioners. Besides, the penalty for murder was not entrenched until after Shem, Ham and Japheth had left the ark and started their own nations.

The punishment was severe for a crime that is the ultimate of evil, but in this Bible verse there is an important message for human societies, past and present.

"By *man* shall his blood be shed." There is a continuous controversy in our society about whether we should or should not have capital punishment. We cannot follow or obey all of the biblical laws and penalties of a past age simply because it is in the Bible and because the LORD or God was said to have commanded it. Remember what Moses did, and how Abraham was told to kill his son. Not all of the lawgivers of the time were moved by the Holy Spirit, regardless if they were prophets, patriarchs or kings. "By their fruits shall you know them," Jesus once said.

However, what Genesis 9:6 is stating is that we have dominion over our planet and have the right and the duty to keep evil under control and protect society. It is our responsibility to give leniency under certain conditions, to rehabilitate if possible, and pass the death sentence for the most heinous and willful crimes. We have the right to play God because we *are* the gods of the world.

> I will be his father, and he shall be to me a son. If he commit iniquity, I will chasten him with the rod of men, and with the stripes of the children of men. 2 Samuel 7:14

> ...for you render to every man according to his work... .
> Psalm 62:12

The Power of Guilt

Adam and Eve chose worldly knowledge over spiritual wisdom, the skins of animals over the silks and linens of the gods and Lords, and the cave instead of paradise. In the first family made in the image of God, there was a murderer and a victim. And from that era to the present day, there have been wars and rumors of wars, but the most intense war of all has been the battle between good and evil.

In the earliest discovered writings of the most ancient Sumerian city of Urak, the poets made their king Gilgamish a folk hero because he symbolized human courage and inspiration in his struggle against evil.

Long before Gilgamish there were the patriarchs who were perfect in their generations and who walked with God. There were the prophets who mediated between God and man, and who warned of the consequences of evil deeds. Then there was the occasional philosopher and king who tried to heal a sick world, and some died for the cause.

As paradise faded into the subconscious and the age of forgetfulness set in, people felt a sense of remorse and a strong need for forgiveness and atonement for sins they didn't understand. They felt inferior and *knew* that they had to sacrifice something of value in order to appease the gods and spirits that could, and did, punish them with the forces of nature.

What was more precious than a human life? Many nations around the world gave to their gods the most valuable part of their lives—their children—on the sacrificial altar, while others traded for slaves and war captives.

The Semite cultures from which the Bible originates were mostly believers of the One God and sacrificed the best of their animals. It was still blood, but at least it wasn't their own or that of their children. God would understand. Except for Abraham, who felt that he should present to God the ultimate gift—his only son. Perhaps the reason that thought entered his mind was because he was born and grew up in the heathen Sumerian city of Ur and sacrificing children may have been common. Other Jews gave to God their animals, but Abraham *thought* that he heard God ask him for his son.

What these nations and various cultures all developed over time was RELIGION! We see the Bible that we have today as a book of religion that has been passed down to us by God, but the true *Word of God* is not religious. Yes, the Bible contains some of the thoughts of God as they were given to men who wrote as they were moved by the Holy Spirit, but it is also full of religion which is not of God. *The Book of the Generations of Adam, The Book of Enoch* and down to *the Testimony* and the Commandments that were placed in the Ark of the Covenant are to teach humankind of this planet about their creation, their purpose on the planet and their place in the universe.

Religion is man-made, and we don't need religion to be in tune with our souls and with God. We do not need someone behind a pulpit to tell us what to wear or what not to wear, how often to pray and where to pray or where we should go to worship. Some people like to gather together in a group and worship and that's fine, as is the one who leads them, but it's not necessary for cosmic union of body and soul. How can one tell what is truth and what isn't? *By their fruits you shall know them.*

> Beware of false prophets which come to you in sheep's clothing, but inwardly they are ravening wolves. You shall know them by their fruits. Do men gather grapes of thorns, or figs of thistles?
>
> Matthew 7:15–16

> ...For you desire not sacrifices...you delight not in burnt offerings.
>
> Psalm 51:16

> ...For what purpose is the multitude of your sacrifices to me... .
>
> Isaiah 1:11

> To do justice and judgement is more acceptable to the LORD than sacrifice. Proverbs 21:3

> For I desired mercy, and not sacrifice; and the knowledge of God more than burnt offerings. Hosea 6:6

> Wherewith shall I come before the LORD, and bow myself before the high God? Shall I come before him with burnt offerings, with calves of a year old? Will the LORD be pleased with thousands of rams, or with ten thousands of rivers of oil? Shall I give my firstborn for my transgressions, the fruit of my body for the sin of my soul? He has shown you, O man, what is good; and what the LORD requires of you, but to do justly, and to love mercy, and to walk humbly with your God. Micah 6:6–8

The Star of Bethlehem

It was said that Caesar Augustus one night consulted his personal sibyl (fortuneteller) and asked her if a prince greater than he would ever be born. As she searched for an answer in her sacred books, the place was lit up by a meteor that flared in the dark sky. She put down her book and told him that he had just received his answer.

"It is a sign of the future which is revealed to you," she said. "One world is ending and another is beginning." What it meant was that the age of Aries the ram had just ended and the age of Pisces the fishes was in.

The sibyl went on to tell Augustus that a child had been born who is the king of future millennia and the true god of the world. "He is of humble birth and obscure race. His divinity is unrealized; when he at last makes himself known, he will be persecuted. He will work miracles, he will be accused of dealing with evil spirits, but I see him victor in the end over death, rising from the place where his murderers entombed him. He will unite all nations."

It is not known whether Augustus believed the sibyl's vision, but it was told to the Roman Senate, recorded and placed in the state archives, from where Constantine drew his information and became a firm believer in astrology.

Every Christmas the Yuletide card portrays a silver star in a navy blue sky and every year the same heavenly object sparkles from the top of the decorated evergreen. At season's end the three wise men and their fellow shepherds gather at a hastily set up manger for the familiar nativity scene.

Though it shimmers on the greeting card and its brilliance lights up the tannebaum, it wasn't a star that erupted into a supernova on that dark Judean night. The star that shone so brightly two thousand years ago was wrapped in swaddling clothes and lying in a manger. "...There shall come a Star out of Jacob, and a Sceptre shall rise out of Israel... ." (Numbers 24:17) The moment that he was born, he lit up the whole world.

The wise men of that era were not the kings of song and legend, but men of renown who counseled kings, and many a crown trembled when they spoke words of doom. They were professional astrologers, mathematicians and clairvoyants, wise to the movements of the stars and the rhythm of the heavens and able to interpret dreams and visions.

The countries that the wise men came from or how many there were is not known, but they brought expensive and lavish gifts of gold, frankincense and myrrh, which is found in Arabia and Eastern Africa. The quality of their gifts can only mean that they were fully aware of the importance of their journey and that this foreign child was somebody very special to the world. There had been prophecies of his coming for centuries and when the sign in the heavens manifested itself, "they came to worship him."

> Now when Jesus was born in Bethlehem of Judaea in the days of Herod the king, behold, there came wise men from the east to Jerusalem, saying, Where is he that is born King of the Jews? For we have seen his star in the east, and are come to worship him.
>
> Matthew 2:1 – 2

The general consensus has been that Jesus was born in the year 6 BC, and there have been heavenly phenomena to support the theory.

One astronomer, Michael Molnar from Rutgers University in New Jersey, after studying star formations and astrological signs on ancient Roman coins and the writings of Ptolemy, discovered that in March 20, 6 BC, the moon occulted Jupiter.

Only a month later a second occultation occurred. Molnar believes that the first one would have signified a major event in astrology which would have sent the wise men on their way to search for the new king, and the second event would have been in the direction of Bethlehem.

To the wise men, this could have been significant, as Jupiter was considered the symbol for kings in Middle East astrology, and Pisces was the *House of the Hebrews*.

Molnar's speculations seem to be the closest of any so far, and places the time of the birth of Jesus only two years before the death of King Herod.

The wise men were warned in a dream not to go back and tell Herod where the child was: "Then Herod, when he saw that he was mocked of the wise men, was exceeding wroth, and sent forth, and slew all the children that were in Bethlehem…from two years and under, according to the time which he had diligently inquired of the wise men." (Matthew 2:16) Herod died shortly after, in March, 4 BC.

The story of the star of Bethlehem doesn't end there. There was that other phenomenon in the sky that has been overlooked by astrologers, astronomers and Bible readers in general.

All of the supernovas, planetary conjunctions, comets and occultations do not fully explain the bright, visible light that led the wise men to the Christ child. Maybe the word *star* was used by translators for something they couldn't explain. It was a bright object which they believed to be a star; and it was, indeed, a very bright light that must have hovered lower than any star.

An astrological sign of the Zodiac in the heavens does not move, is barely visible to the naked eye, and is not noticed at all by someone who does not know what to look for. The astrologers saw "his star [zodiac sign] in the east" and that was where it remained when they set out on their journey. They were then led by something that *did* move, however, and it brought them in the direction of Jerusalem.

While they were speaking to king Herod, the star that led them apparently vanished. Otherwise they could have shown him their star in the night sky, but he inquired instead of the sign that they had seen in the east. After they had left the king's presence and departed,

> the star, which they saw in the east, went before them, till it came and stood over where the young child was. When they saw the star, they rejoiced with exceeding great joy. And when they were come into the house, they saw the young child with Mary his mother, and fell down and worshipped him. . . . Matthew 2:9–11

Supernovas, conjunctions and comets don't perform stunts like that. Some of our neighbors in the cosmos were aware of the blessed event in our world and, as a friendly gesture, escorted the men of renown to meet the Lord of Lords.

It also explains why the shepherds in Luke's account of the nativity (Luke 2) did not see a star in the sky on the night of the birth. Shepherds who have to stay awake to tend to their sheep would surely have seen a spectacular star if it had suddenly flashed above them. Instead, they were treated to a psychic experience. "And lo, the angel of the Lord came upon them, and the glory of the Lord shone round about them: and they were sore afraid. And the angel said unto them, Fear not: for, behold, I bring you good tidings of great joy, which shall be to all people. For unto you is born this day in the city of David a Saviour, which is Christ the Lord."

"Glory to God in the Highest and on earth peace, good will toward men."

> And, behold, there was a man in Jerusalem, whose name was Simeon, and the same man was just and devout. . . and it was revealed unto him by the Holy Ghost, that he should not see death, before he had seen the Lord's Christ. Luke 2:25–26

Throughout the history of the tribes of Jacob, Jehovah was their Lord and their God. As do all Lords of the heavenly host, he spoke for God and as God the Supreme and the Almighty. He was the Lord of God who was ordained to care for and guide the people who were chosen to bring forth into this world the Son of God.

The Son of man would come through the seed of David, and the Lord God Jehovah would hand over to him the throne of his forefather David. He was the Christ of all the Lords and the Son of the Highest.

And the angel Gabriel said to Mary:

> You shall conceive in your womb, and bring forth a son, and shall call his name JESUS. He shall be great, and shall be called the Son of the Highest: and the Lord God shall give unto him the throne of his father David. And he shall reign over the house of Jacob forever; and of his kingdom there shall be no end. Luke 1:30–33

When Jesus was born, they came from near and far to worship him. There were the Jews (shepherds) and the Gentiles (wise men). There were the illiterate, and those who read the stars, the poor who tended their sheep on the hillside, and the rich who counseled kings in their palaces.

Why did he come?

There are many waters throughout the universe, more than can be numbered. Has he visited all of them? He is the Lord of the worlds and cosmos and perhaps when a world becomes conscious of its humanity, he comes and teaches each one personally the cosmic union of body and soul. Many of the waters would welcome him as a revered guest on their home planet, and there would be some, like ours, that would have him murdered.

From the beginning of our evolution, there has been constant war and rumors of war. There is turmoil and discord, and there seems to be only evil continually. We have been sent many prophets and saints, and most of them we have killed. Two thousand years ago, the Son of man and God paid us a visit to finally bring us peace and good will to all humankind. His message was very simple:

> Come to me, all of you who labour and are heavy laden, and I will give you rest. Take my yoke upon you, and learn of me; for I am

> meek and lowly in heart: and you shall find rest for your souls. For my yoke is easy, and my burden is light. Matthew 11:28–30

The Jewish nation had reasons to rejoice. From their beginnings they were constantly at war, or captives of other countries.

> The people that walked in darkness have seen a great light: they shall dwell in the land of the shadow of death, upon them has the light shined...For unto us a child is born, unto us a son is given: and the government shall be upon his shoulder: and his name shall be called Wonderful, Counsellor, The Mighty God, The Everlasting Father, The Prince of Peace.... Isaiah 9:2–6

The Gentiles of the whole world, they would become as his adopted sons:

> The people which sat in darkness saw a great light; and to them which sat in the region and the shadow of death light is sprung up. Matthew 4:16

The world in general, however, rejected him:

> The kings of the earth stood up, and the rulers were gathered together against the Lord, and against his Christ. Acts 4:26

They crucified him, one of the most horrid, brutal and evil acts a human could conjure up in his imagination:

> ...the assembly of the wicked have enclosed me: they pierced my hands and my feet...They part my garments among them, and cast lots upon my vesture. Psalm 22:16–18

Before he was led to his death, he described the temple as a metaphor for his body:

> We heard him say, I will destroy this temple made with hands, and within three days I will build another made without hands. Mark 14:58

> Jesus answered and said to them, Destroy this temple, and in three days I will raise it up. Then said the Jews, Forty and six years was this temple in building, and you will raise it up in three days? But he spoke of the temple of his body. John 2:19–21

> And it was about the sixth hour, and there was darkness over all the earth until the ninth hour. And the sun was darkened, and the face of the temple was rent through the middle. Luke 23:45

The Beginning of Sorrows

From the earliest of times, and maybe even as early as Adam, the mental giants and men of renown noticed that in the night sky there was a pattern to the stars and order in the heavens. Their mathematical minds went to work and somewhere and sometime in that distant past, the Zodiac was established in cultures around the world.

Astrology was the original astronomy, and blended in with it was prophecy and clairvoyance. Most astrologers of the time were also seers, as was Abraham, who was well known for his ability in counseling kings, and Moses, the greatest of them all, who learned his craft in an Egyptian palace.

It was during these ages that our Bible evolved, and throughout the scriptures in both the Old and New Testaments the *signs of the times* are prominent.

In astrology, a *Great Year* is the time it takes the planet to pass through the Twelve Signs of the Zodiac. This is 25,868 years, but there is no clear line between each sign, which is called *a Great Month* and lasts approximately 2000 years and a little beyond that. For simplicity, the months are calculated at the beginning and end of each millennium.

The night that Jesus was born, apparently the Age of Aries the ram ended and the Age of Pisces the fishes began. Aries was the age of battle. It was a war-saturated age and the Jewish tribes of the time were no exception. They were as bloodthirsty as they were religious and the *chosen* people of Israel, from whose lineage Jesus would come, were inclined to forget their LORD on occasion and worship the ram.

In the Age of Pisces, Christianity was born and the awareness of humility and charity. The early Christians used the symbol of the fishes scratched on the walls of their secret hiding places for other Christians during the Roman persecution, and Jesus referred to his disciples as "fishers of men." In the Age of Pisces, the struggle has been for freedom from war and persecution—and a struggle it has been—especially between good and evil.

When Jesus spoke of the Jewish temple, of his body, and how both would be destroyed, it was also meant as a sign of the times. That dark and terrible night there was an earthquake and the temple was rent down the middle. His physical body was dead, and the Age of Pisces became the Beginning of Sorrows.

For two days Jesus was in the grave. He brought in the Age of Pisces of *Peace on earth and good will to all*, but for "two days" and two thousand years (the Age of Pisces) there would be no peace or good will while his spirit was gone from our presence.

In God's time, one day is as a thousand years, and a thousand years as one day.

> Take heed that no man deceive you. For many shall come in my name, saying, I am Christ; and shall deceive many. And you shall hear of wars and rumours of wars: see that you be not troubled: for all these things must come to pass, but the end is not yet. For nation shall rise against nation, and kingdom against kingdom: and there shall be famines, and pestilences, and earthquakes, in divers places. All these are the beginning of sorrows [The Age of Pisces]. Then shall they deliver you up to be afflicted, and shall kill you: and you shall be hated of all nations for my name's sake. And then shall many be offended, and shall betray one another, and shall hate one another. And many false prophets shall rise, and shall deceive many. And because iniquity shall abound, the love of many shall [become] cold. But he that shall endure unto the end, the same shall be saved. And this gospel of the kingdom shall be preached in all the world for a witness unto all nations; and then shall the end come.
>
> Matthew 24:4–14

> For many shall come in my name, saying, I am Christ; and deceive many...and there shall be earthquakes...and there shall be famines and troubles: these are the beginnings of sorrows...And the gospel

> must first be published among all nations...Now brother shall betray brother to death, and the father the son; and children shall rise up against their parents, and shall cause them to be put to death. And you shall be hated of all men for my name's sake....
>
> Mark 13:6–13

This age of sorrows not only pertains to the world in general, but there is also a special message for the Jews:

> And when you shall see Jerusalem compassed with armies, then know that the desolation thereof is nigh. Then let them which are in Judaea flee to the mountains; and let them which are in the midst of it depart out; and let not them that are in the countries enter thereinto. For these be the days of vengeance, that all things that are written may be fulfilled. But woe unto them that are with child, and to them that nurse, in those days! For there shall be great distress in the land, and wrath upon this people. And they shall fall by the edge of the sword, and shall be led away captive into all nations: and Jerusalem shall be trodden down of the Gentiles, until the times of the Gentiles be fulfilled. Luke 21:20–24

> O Jerusalem, Jerusalem, you who kill the prophets, and stone them which are sent to you, how often would I have gathered your children together, even as a hen gathers her chicks under her wing, and you would not! Behold, your house is left to you desolate. For I say to you, You shall not see me henceforth, till you shall say, Blessed is he that comes in the name of the Lord. Matthew 23:37–39

> And I say to you, That many shall come from the east and west, and shall sit down with Abraham, Isaac, and Jacob, in the kingdom of heaven. But the children of the kingdom shall be cast out into outer darkness; there shall be weeping and gnashing of teeth.
>
> Matthew 8:11–12

The Son of man was put through a physical death by the forces of evil, but the seed of the serpent only managed to "bruise his heel." The world can never destroy evil, as it is a dimension of God, but we can "bruise its head" and keep it under control.

For two thousand years (two days), our world has been torn down the middle, like the temple, between good and evil and we have been spiritually dead like the body of Christ, but the third day is dawning! It is the spiritual resurrection of the Son of God, and there will be peace on earth and good will to all.

The time has come and it is *NOW*! It is *NOT* the end of the world as many people fear and the messengers of doom have prophesied. On the contrary, it is the beginning of a New World Order. Jesus will be King of kings and Lord of Lords, not in body, but in the Spirit of God.

In astrology, it is known as the Age of Aquarius.

The Age of Aquarius

> The normal Aquarian preoccupation with rational science is clearly seen in the way that our civilization is becoming increasingly based on, and dominated by science and technology. However, the keyword of Aquarius is 'humanity' and in the future it is to be hoped that this quality will modify the present over emphasis on science, harnessing it more to the actual needs of man, than simply to what is technically possible. The moderating influence of Aquarius' polarity with Leo will also be needed to avert the dangers of revolution, and reinforce the growing concern for peace.[3]

> Daniel: I saw in the night visions, and, behold, one like the Son of man came with the clouds of heaven…And there was given him dominion, and glory, and a kingdom, that all people, nations and languages, should serve him: his dominion is an everlasting dominion, which shall not pass away, and his kingdom that which shall not be destroyed. Daniel 7:13 – 14

> And it shall be in that day, that living waters shall go out from Jerusalem…And the LORD shall be king over all the earth: in that day shall there be one LORD, and his name one.
>
> Zechariah 14:8 – 9

> For the earth shall be filled with the knowledge of the glory of the LORD, as the waters cover the sea. Habakkuk 2:14

> And many nations shall come, and say, Come, let us go up to the mountain of the LORD, and to the house of the God of Jacob; and he will teach us his ways, and we will walk in his paths: for the law shall go forth of Zion, and the word of the LORD from Jerusalem. And he shall judge among many people, and rebuke strong nations afar off; and they shall beat their swords into plowshares, and their spears into pruning hooks: nation shall not lift up a sword against nation, neither shall they learn war anymore. Micah 4:2–3

> For the LORD shall comfort Zion…he will make her wilderness like Eden, and her desert like the garden of the LORD; joy and gladness shall be found therein, thanksgiving, and the voice of melody. Isaiah 51:3

All of these prophecies were written thousands of years ago by prophets who walked with God, and now their words are about to become reality. We have experienced wars and rumors of wars, famines and natural catastrophes, but finally, after two thousand years of sorrows, peace and good will are close at hand.

> Take heed that no man deceive you…these are the beginnings of sorrows, but the end is not yet…and the gospel of the kingdom shall be preached in all the world for a witness unto all nations, and then shall the end come… . Matthew 24:4–14

The Gospel of the Kingdom

What is the gospel of the kingdom? The kingdom of heaven/God is *within us*. The human soul was designed in the image and likeness of God to be in communion with the Almighty Energy and Light. We have a choice, however, and that too is human. We can be apart from God and be spiritually dead or we can be a part *of* God and be alive in spirit. One is knowledge from the brain and the other is wisdom from the soul.

The gospel of wisdom was the tree of life in the center of the garden of Eden that Adam and Eve could not fully comprehend the meaning of, and it was the message that Jesus brought to our planet again two thousand years ago. And we still did not understand. His own people condemned him to death and the Gentiles nailed him to the cross.

Our planet has been given another chance to become a paradise on earth, but for that to happen we have to be "born again," as Jesus said. As we were born in the body, so we must also be reborn in the spirit, in cosmic union of body and soul. To be fully alive we can't have one without the other, and that is the gospel of the kingdom.

When and how will this New Age begin?

It has already begun. There still are wars and calamities beyond imagination, but there is also an awakening of souls long dead and a longing for spiritual wisdom. There is a growing awareness of the power of *thought* and how it can affect the body and soul, whether for good or evil, and we are questioning the purpose in life. Is there a purpose?

Over the course of time, our planet will discover its role in the cosmos, but the most profound change will occur in the nation where the physical birth of Jesus took place. From this nation the ruler of the New Age will be born, and he will set the world on its path toward peace and good will to all. No, it is not Jesus, but a servant of the Lord of Lords, endowed with the spirit of the Prince of Peace.

In the Old Testament book of Zechariah, the prophet is told by an angel of the LORD that the soul of Joshua, who was once a high priest, would be sent forth to be the Lord's servant known as *the BRANCH*.

> Then take silver and gold, and make crowns, and set them upon the head of Joshua the son of Josedech, the high priest; And speak unto him, saying, Thus will speak the LORD of hosts, saying, Behold the man whose name is The BRANCH; and he shall grow up out of his place, and he shall build the temple of the LORD...and he shall bear the glory, and shall sit and rule upon his throne: and he shall be a priest upon his throne: and the counsel of peace shall be between them both. Zechariah 6:11–13

> And there shall come forth a rod out of the stem of Jesse, and a Branch shall grow out of his roots: And the spirit of the LORD shall rest upon him, the spirit of wisdom and understanding, the spirit of counsel and might, the spirit of knowledge and of the fear of the LORD; And shall make him of quick understanding in the fear of the LORD: and he shall not judge after the sight of his eyes, neither reprove after the hearing of his ears: But with righteousness shall he judge the poor, and reprove with equity for the meek of the earth: and he shall smite the earth with the rod of his mouth [sharp words], and with the breath of his lips shall he slay the wicked. And righteousness shall be the girdle of his loins, and faithfulness the girdle of his reins. The wolf also shall dwell with the lamb, and the leopard shall lie down with the kid; and the calf and the young lion and the fatling together; and a little child shall lead them. And the cow and the bear shall feed; their young ones shall lie down together; and the lion shall eat straw like the ox. And the nursing child shall play on the hole of the asp, and the weaned child shall put his hand on the cockatrice's den. They shall not hurt nor destroy in all my holy mountain: for the earth shall be full of the knowledge of the LORD, as the waters cover the sea. And in that day there shall be a root of Jesse, which shall stand for an ensign of the people: to it shall the Gentiles seek: and his rest shall be glorious. And it shall come to pass in that day, that the Lord shall set his hand again the second time to recover the remnant of his people.... Isaiah 11

> And God said, Behold, I have given you every herb bearing seed...every tree in which is the fruit...to you it shall be for meat. And to every beast of the earth, and to every fowl of the air, and to every thing that creeps upon the earth, wherein there is life, I have given every green herb for meat, and it was so. Genesis 1:29–30

The Son of God brought us back to paradise on earth—physically, mentally and spiritually. In the New Age, beginning with the Age of Aquarius, the message of the kingdom of God and heaven that is within us will be preached and taught throughout the world, and it will go on for eons of time.

From Adam to Jesus there was the law: "For Christ is the end of the law... ." (Romans 10:4)

> Think not that I am come to destroy the law, or the prophets: I am not come to destroy, but to fulfil. For verily I say unto you, Till heaven and earth pass, one jot or one mark shall in no wise pass from the law, till all be fulfilled. Matthew 5:17–18

> ...and of his kingdom there shall be no end... . Luke 1:33

It will last as long as the breath of God, during the continued expansion of the cosmos, and through the contraction, near to the point of zero. "...and then shall the end come." (Matthew 24:14) Remember, this is NOT the return of Jesus, but rather of the spirit of Jesus through the reincarnation of Joshua, The BRANCH.

The End of Time: The Tribulation

The scriptures in both the Old and the New Testaments tend to run the Age of Sorrows and The Tribulation together, and that has caused confusion and misinterpretation within the Christian denominations. It has resulted in false prophesies concerning the end of the world and the Second Coming of Christ; and No, the world is not going to end just yet, and Jesus is not coming back in a physical body again—ever! Nor is the Second Coming going to take place next week, next month, or ten years from now.

Because religion and science have never been the best of friends, the Bible's account of the beginning and ending of the heavens and the earth has never been associated with science's theory of the expansion and contraction of the universe.

> Jesus said to his initiates: "...which I will one day tell you when I come to speak of that mystery, that is when I shall have told you of the expansion of the universe. Albeit at the dissolution of the universe, that is when the number of the perfect souls would be completed and the mystery through which the universe altogether has risen is completed... ."[4]

> He has compassed the waters with bounds, until the day and night come to an end. Job 26:10

(In the Bible, Day and Night have many interpretations. Day: light; knowledge; salvation; a beginning of time. Night: darkness, ignorance or evil; death; ending of a day or time period.)

> The mighty God, even the LORD, has spoken, and called the earth from the rising of the sun to the going down thereof. Psalm 50:1

Our planet is nearing the end of the Age of Sorrows, and a New Age of peace and good will is beginning. The first spiritual ruler of this era will be born (if he hasn't already) in the new Zion and will be a BRANCH from Jesse, the father of king David of biblical times. He will rule the world in the *spirit* of Christ, and evil will be chained for the duration of the Age.

> And I saw a great angel come down from heaven, having the key of the bottomless pit and a great chain in his hand. And he laid hold on the dragon, that old serpent, which is the Devil, and Satan, and bound him a thousand years, And cast him into the bottomless pit, and shut him up, and set a seal upon him, that he should deceive the nations no more, till the thousand years should be fulfilled: and after that he must be loosed a little season. Revelation 20:1 – 3

If one of our days is as a thousand years of the Light, one thousand years of the Light would be, in our time in the New Age, 36,500,000 years. I don't think we will have to concern ourselves with the tribulation or the end of the cosmos just yet.

After the thousand years of Light (God's time), evil will be "loosed a little season," and it will be similar to the Age of Sorrows in many ways. This tribulation is a natural process of the cosmos as it draws near to its contraction to zero. The lowest part of God will manifest itself as the matter in the universe deteriorates like a worn out garment. Hell is the fiery pit of antimatter that will destroy matter back to nothing. It is the ultimate of Black Holes.

> Then let them which be in Judaea flee to the mountains: Let him which is on the housetop not come down to take anything out of his house: Neither let him which is in the field turn back to take his clothes...For then shall be great tribulation, such as was not since the beginning of the world to this time, no, nor ever shall be. And except these days should be shortened, there should no flesh be saved: but for the elect's sake those days shall be shortened.
>
> Matthew 24:16–22

The tribulation was also known as the battle between good and evil:

> For they are the spirits of devils, working miracles unto the kings of the earth and of the whole world, to gather them to the battle of that great day of God Almighty...And he gathered them together into a place called in the Hebrew tongue Armageddon. And the seventh angel poured out his vial into the air, and there came a great voice out of the temple of heaven, from the throne, saying, It is done. And there were voices, and thunders, and lightenings; and there was a great earthquake, such as was not since men were upon the earth, so mighty an earthquake, and so great.
>
> Revelation 16:14–18

> Immediately after the tribulation of those days shall the sun be darkened, and the moon shall not give her light, and the stars shall fall from heaven, and the powers of the heavens shall be shaken: And then shall appear the sign of the Son of man in heaven: and then shall all of the tribes of the earth mourn, and they shall see the Son of man coming in the clouds of heaven with power and great glory. And he shall send his angels with a great sound of a trumpet, and they shall gather together his elect from the four winds, from one end of heaven to the other...Verily, I say unto you, This generation [one breath of God] shall not pass, till all these things be fulfilled. Heaven and earth shall pass away, but my words shall not pass away. But of that day and hour knows no man, no, not the angels of heaven, but my Father only. But as the days of Noah were, so also shall the coming of the Son of man be...Then shall two be

in the field; the one shall be taken and the other left. Two women shall be grinding at the mill; the one shall be taken, and the other left. Watch therefore: for you know not what hour your Lord will come. Matthew 24:29–42

Therefore I will shake the heavens, and the earth shall remove out of her place.... Isaiah 13:13

The earth is utterly broken down, the earth is clean dissolved, the earth is moved exceedingly. The earth shall reel to and fro like a drunkard, and shall be removed like a cottage; and the transgression thereof shall be heavy upon it; and it shall fall, and not rise again. Isaiah 24:19–20

And all the host of heaven shall be dissolved, and the heavens shall be rolled together as a scroll: and all their host shall fall down, as the leaf falls off from the vine, and as a falling fig from the fig tree. Isaiah 34:4

Lift up your eyes to the heavens, and look upon the earth beneath: for the heavens shall vanish away like smoke, and the earth shall grow old like a garment, and they that dwell therein shall die in like manner: but my salvation shall be forever, and my righteousness shall not be abolished. Isaiah 51:6

The sun shall be turned into darkness, and the moon into blood, before the great and the terrible day of the LORD come. And it shall come to pass, that whosoever shall call on the name of the LORD shall be delivered: for in mount Zion and in Jerusalem shall be deliverance, as the LORD has said, and in the remnant whom the LORD shall call. Joel 2:31–32

The earth will once again be without form, and void, and darkness will be upon the face of the deep.

Then, another breath from the Energy and the Light, as the Spirit of God moves upon the face of the waters, and the souls of the elect will return.

> And I saw a new heaven and a new earth: for the first heaven and the first earth were passed away: and there was no more sea [space].
> Revelation 21:1

> For, behold, I create new heavens and a new earth: and the former shall not be remembered, nor come to mind. Isaiah 65:17

With each breath of God, which is one expansion and contraction of the cosmos, there is a renewal of matter (new heavens and earth) to accommodate the new and returned souls and spirits of all that has life.

We have all lived from the time that mankind became living souls in human bodies, whenever and wherever it was in the universe. Some of us existed in the former cosmos or ones before that, but we don't remember them, nor do they come to mind.

Neither do all of our past lives during this lifespan come to mind, as we are born into one body after another. When one body can no longer sustain life, the soul moves on into another newborn, over and over until the contraction of the cosmos once again.

Some of us were there when Jesus was nailed to the cross, and one of us may have pierced his side to make sure that he was dead. Some of us will be alive at the moment when he returns in the clouds to gather his elect. Not all will believe in a conscious God or in the Word that was given to us in the beginning. Not all will accept the spirit of wisdom or the kingdom of heaven that is within us, and their names will not be "in the book of life from the foundation of the world." (Revelation 17:8)

> For the Son of man shall come in the glory of his Father with his angels, and then he shall reward every man according to his works. Verily I say unto you, There be some standing here, which shall not taste death, till they see the Son of man coming in his kingdom.
> Matthew 16:27–28

> Behold, he comes with clouds; and every eye shall see him, and they also which pierced him: and all kindreds of the earth shall wail because of him. Even so, Amen. I am Alpha and Omega, the

> beginning and the ending, says the Lord, which is, and which was, and which is to come, the Almighty. Revelation 1:7–8

> The Lord is not slack concerning his promise, as some men count slackness; but is longsuffering toward us, not willing that any should perish, but that all should come to repentance. But the day of the Lord will come as a thief in the night; in which the heavens shall pass away with a great noise, and the elements shall melt with fervent heat, the earth also and the works that are therein shall be burned up. 2 Peter 3:9–10

> For the Lord himself shall descend from heaven with a shout, with the voice of the archangel, and with the trump of God: and the dead in Christ shall rise first: then we which are alive and remain shall be caught up together with them in the clouds, to meet the Lord in the air: and so shall we ever be with the Lord.
> 1 Thessalonians 4:16–17

> And I saw the dead, small and great, stand before God; and the books were opened: and another book was opened, which is the book of life: and the dead were judged out of those things which were written in the books, according to their works. And the sea [space; the waters] gave up the dead which were in it; and death and hell delivered up the dead which were in them: and they were judged every man according to their works. And death and hell were cast into the lake of fire. This is the second death. And whosoever was not found written in the book of life was cast into the lake of fire. Revelation 20:12–15

During one cycle of the expansion and contraction of the cosmos, each one of us will have gone through many physical deaths, but in biblical terms they are only counted as one, which it refers to as the first death. At the end of the cycle, those who have chosen not to be one with God in spirit will go through the second death and their souls will be annihilated back to basic energy, along with the rest of the cosmos. The pit, or lake of fire, is the end-all and the brief moment before the next breath of God. It is a natural process of the Energy and the Light: the Black Hole of God.

The many reincarnations that we experience are just one life's story with many chapters. Some chapters are of a long life, well into old age, and some last only a few days, or minutes, and every minute is entered into a *book*.

During each life's chapter, we have within our souls the dimension of the kingdom of God/heaven and hell, and when we reach the age where we can understand the knowledge of good and evil, we have a choice. If a soul chooses evil in thought and deed, upon death of the body that soul will be in the level of their chosen hell. This hell, however, is not the *lake of fire*. It is a state of mind and a condition of the soul, and it is not permanent. Even while in this hell, a soul can ask for forgiveness and a change of venue, and that is what the Bible refers to as salvation.

Just as the physical body needs its nutrients in order to stay alive, the soul needs the kingdom of God and heaven. Without this nourishment from the Spirit, the soul will eventually die a natural death in the lake of fire at the end of time.

The Word of God

The Word of God, from the beginning, was to teach us how to be *sons of God* and how to save our souls at the end of time. From the beginning, it was made into a religion—strict and unyielding and instilled with fear. Later, when the Lord of Lords brought the message of peace and good will to all, he stated that in order for there to be peace and good will, and to enter into the *rest*, we must be *born again* in cosmic union of body and soul.

His followers and apostles made that, too, into a religion. Being born again or being converted is NOT a religious concept, nor was it intended to be. It is a way of life—The only way to live a healthy and productive life!

It should be included in every medical textbook and in Psychology 101. We are made up of spirit, soul and body, and *conversion* means we have to include the spiritual mode into our lives instead of a worldly one. We are made in the likeness of God and are a part of God. He is, in essence, our Father, and as a child does with a kind and loving father, we must have faith and trust in the Almighty God in order to be healthy, wealthy and wise.

There are no laws or rituals that must be adhered to from a church, temple or synagogue, and one does not have to stand up in an audience and give testimony or "do alms before men to be seen of them."

"...And when you pray...enter into your closet [privacy], and when you have shut the door, pray to your Father which is in secret, and your Father which is in secret shall reward you openly... ." (Matthew 6).

Prayer is not for schools, assembly halls or government offices. It is a private moment between the soul and its Father, and there should be no interference.

True conversion is not made up of testimonies to prove to others that one is headed for heaven, and there are no repetitive and memorized prayers or shouts from the rooftops. It is a candle that shines without a sound and is fed by the thoughts and deeds of God. That is the kingdom of heaven.

To have faith and trust in God does not mean a blind belief and acceptance of everyone that calls himself a servant of God, and neither is it an acceptance of every word in the Bible. By its fruit you shall know the tree.

Solomon, in all his wisdom, declared that a child should be beaten with a blunt object to save its soul from hell. (Proverbs 23). He assured the parents that their child would not die. Well, yes, Solomon, a child could die and some have died, and a part of the child's spirit *does* die in the process.

> Jesus said, "Whoever offends [hurts] one of these little ones...it were better for him that a millstone were hanged about his neck, and that he were drowned in the depth of the sea." Matthew 18:6

> But the anointing which you have received of him abides in you, and you need not that any man teach you: but as the same anointing [Spirit of God] teaches you of all things, and is truth, and is no lie, and even as it has taught you, you shall abide in him. 1 John 2:27

We are *sons of God*, the Spirit of Energy and Light, and we are also *sons of men* born of Mother Earth. From them we *live and move and have our being*. We are the children of the cosmos, and there are more of us than there is *sand upon the seashore*. We are all of *one blood, and our hearts are made alike*. Within a vast universe beyond human comprehension, in the central sphere of God, our worlds are as *isles in the sea* and *as fountains of the deep*. In the Word of God they are known as *The Many Waters*!

The fool has said in his heart, There is no God. Psalm 14:1

NOTES

[1] Mead, G.R.S. (1974). *Pistis Sophia*. Secaucus, NJ: University Books Inc., p. 27.

[2] Budge, E.A.W. (1960). *The Book of the Dead*. New York, NY: University Books, The Papyrus of ANI.

[3] Parker, J. & Parker, D. (1971). *The Compleat Astrologer*. New York, NY: McGraw-Hill Publishers, p. 45.

[4] Mead, G.R.S. (1974). *Pistis Sophia*. Secaucus, NJ: University Books Inc., p.202.

Index

A

B

C

N

P

R

S

T

Permissions

Excerpts from *The Book of Jasher* reprinted by permission of the *The Book of Jasher*©, Supreme Grand Lodge, Rosicrucian Order, AMORC, San Jose, California 95191 U.S.A.

Excerpts from *Pistis Sophia* by G.R.S. Mead, G.R.S. (1974). Secaucus, New Jersey: University Books Inc., reprinted by permission of Roger A. Kessinger, Kessinger Publishing, LLC, P.O. Box 160, Kila, Montana 59920 U.S.A. Phone: (406) 756•0167; Fax: (406) 257•5051; E-mail: books@kessinger.net; Internet: http://www.kessinger.net

DESIGN NOTES

The text of this book has been set in Frederic W. Goudy's 1931 *Truesdell* typeface from **Monotype Typeography**. This unique and intriguing font was lost in a 1939 fire and was recently digitized by Steve Matteson of Monotype from proofs of the 16-point hot metal fonts which reside at Rochester Institute of Technology.

Chapter titles, running heads and page numbers are set in *Quantum* from the **Creative Alliance Library**. The hieroglyph (ooo) appearing in the text, is from *Hieroglyphic Phonetic*, a font created by the **P22 Type Foundary**, and represents "grains of sand".

The hieroglyphs used to create the logo for *Rosetta Stone Press* are also from P22's *Hieroglyphic Phonetic* and *Hieroglyphic Decorative* fonts. The hieroglyph (𓈗) represents "water" and ([hieroglyph]) means "he who carries the ritual book".